A-level Study Guide

Physical Education and Sport

Michael Hill

Revision Express

Series Consultants: Geoff Black and Stuart Wall

Pearson Education Limited

Edinburgh Gate, Harlow

Essex CM20 2JE, England

www.pearsoned.co.uk

and Associated Companies throughout the world

British Library Cataloguing-in-Publication Data

A catalogue entry for this title is available from the British Library.

ISBN 10: 1-405-80170-0
ISBN 13: 978-1-405-80170-6

Second impression 2006
Set by 35 in Univers, Cheltenham

Printed by Ashford Colour Press Ltd, Gosport

Anatomy and physiology

In this chapter we revise the anatomy and physiology of the human body with reference to exercise and movement. Traditionally this is one of the most difficult areas of the exam and needs thorough revision. The main focus should be on the systems that play a significant role in producing movement on the body – the skeletal, muscular, cardiovascular and respiratory systems. Some of the A-level specifications also require candidates to study fitness testing and training and you will find revision sheets for these in the chapter on Exercise Physiology. The key to exam success in the section is first having a thorough understanding of the structure and function of the key body parts and systems but you also need to apply your points to sporting examples.

Exam themes

→ The structure and function of the skeletal system

→ The structure of muscles and their role in creating movement

→ Movement production and control

→ The structure and function of the cardiovascular system

→ The role of blood in transporting oxygen and carbon dioxide

→ The structure and role of the respiratory system

Topic checklist

AS ○ A2 ●

	AQA	EDEXCEL	OCR	WJEC
The skeletal and muscular system	○	○	○	○
Motion and movement	○	○	○	○
The cardiovascular system	○	○	○	○
The role of blood in transporting oxygen and carbon dioxide	○	○	○	○
The respiratory system	○	○	○	○

The skeletal and muscular system

The human skeleton is made up of a combination of bones, joints and cartilage, it has two parts, an **axial** or central part and an **appendicular** part which are attached to the central axial skeleton.

The functions of the skeleton include:

→ provides **shape**; supports body in correct **posture**; **supports** the internal organs; enables us to make **movements**; **protects** the body.

→ sites of **muscle attachment**; creates **levers**; **produces** blood cells.

Joints ●●●

The reasons we are able to move when we play sport is because of our joints, specifically in sport the movable synovial joints. You need to be able to describe and discuss the types of movement that can occur at the following joints.

→ Wrist   Radio-ulnar   Elbow   Shoulder
→ Spine   Hip   Knee   Ankle

Synovial joints allow a great range of movement, formed where a fluid-filled cavity surrounds the meeting of two bones, the ends of which are coated with articular cartilage which acts as a shock absorber.

Ligaments of tough, inelastic connective tissue hold the bones together. They act to prevent any unwanted movement. Tendons, made of fibrous connective tissue, attach the muscles to the bones.

Joints can undergo a number of different movements – you will need to understand the meaning of each movement type as well as being able to apply these to a range of sporting activities as well as identifying the range of movements possible at each joint.

Movement term	Description
Flexion	Decrease in angle between the two bones
Extention	Increase in the angle between two bones
Abduction	Movement of a limb away from an imaginary vertical line down the middle of the body
Adduction	Movement of a limb towards the imaginary mid-line of the body
Rotation	Circular movement
Circumduction	A combination of flexion, extention, abduction, adduction and rotation

Action point

See if you can give a sporting example for each of the movement types identified. If the skeleton provides the framework of the body it is the actual muscles that enable us to maintain our body position and to move our body parts.

Checkpoint 1

What characteristics of synovial joints allow a great range of movement?

Checkpoint 2

Explain the differing roles of ligaments and tendons.

Checkpoint 3

Describe four functions of the human skeleton.

Muscles and movement ●●●

Muscle tissue has four main characteristics:

excitability
contractility
extensibility
elasticity.

This means that muscles

→ react to a stimulus
→ contract and apply force
→ stretch and return to their original length
→ have involuntary control.

Triceps — Biceps
Agonist Antagonist

Muscles can be classified according to the fibre arrangement around the tendon as follows:

→ **Fusiform** – where the fibres run the length of the muscle, a type of muscle designed for mobility.
→ **Pennate** – where the fibres are structured in a fan shape, a type of muscle designed for strength.

Each actual muscle consists of a bundle of fibres contained by a layer of connective tissue known as the epimysium. Its role is to protect the muscle and help it slide smoothly past nearby muscles, bones and other organs as it changes in length.

Inside the epimysium, the muscle is further grouped into bundles, each of these is divided by thinner layers of connective tissue containing blood vessels and nerve fibres.

Skeletal muscle has a striped appearance due to the microscopic fibres called myofibrils which they contain. These myofibrils are made up of alternating rows of two basic protein filaments called actin and myosin, which resemble the teeth of interlocking combs. According to the sliding filament theory, small projections on the myosin filaments allow the protein filaments to slide past each other as the muscle changes in length.

Checkpoint 4

What is the role of the epimysium surrounding the muscle fibres?

Exam question answer: page 14

Explain how the functions of the skeleton facilitate physical activity.

(8 minutes)

Motion and movement

If the skeletal system creates a framework for the body, it is the muscles that maintain our body shape and enable us to move our body parts, they are therefore extremely important when we play sport.

The structure of skeletal muscle ●●●

Muscles are usually attached to two or more different bones so that when they contract movement occurs. Fibrous connective tissues called tendons attach muscles to bones at sites called the point of **origin** and the point of **insertion**. Where a muscle is attached to a bone, a lever system is formed.

A feature of muscle fibres is that they can contract, or pull, against the skeleton. Most muscles are long and thin, but when they contract they get **shorter** and **thicker** – this is called concentric contraction. What muscles cannot do is push, because muscles cannot push. To make joints work, the muscles are arranged in pairs called **antagonistic pairs**. The best example of antagonistic pairs of muscles are the biceps and triceps. At the elbow, in order to bend the arm, the **biceps** contract (shorten) while the **triceps** relax (lengthen).

There are two other connected terms which you should know:

1 Fixators are any other muscles situated near the point of origin of the prime mover, which act to stabilise the body part, so that only the end at the point of insertion will move.
2 Synergists are any other muscle actively working to help the prime mover to cause a movement.

The study of muscles in sport is mainly focussed when they are in a state of contraction. This can happen in a number of different ways. Concentric contraction can occur when a muscle shortens in length and develops tension. Eccentric contraction involves the development of tension while the muscle is being lengthened. Isometric contraction occurs when the muscle develops tension but does not change in length. Finally isokinetic contraction is a special situation in which the muscle is changing in length but at a constant rate.

Skeletal muscle is further divided into three main fibre types:

Type	Description
Type I (slow oxidative)	A type of muscle fibre characterised by a relatively slow contraction, making it suitable for low-power and long-duration activities usually referred to as aerobic.
Type IIa (fast oxidative glycolytic or FOG)	Have a higher oxidative capacity than type IIb and are often associated with short high-intensity endurance events such as the 400m in athletics.
Type IIb (fast glycolytic or FG)	Have the highest level of phosphocreatine and special enzymes, giving the highest glycolytic capacity and are associated with explosive events such as the start of the 100m sprint start.

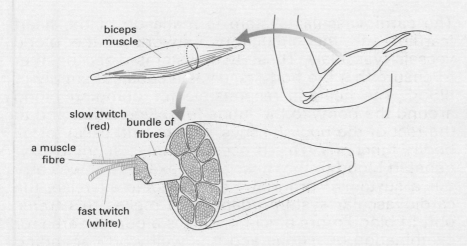

biceps muscle

slow twitch (red)

bundle of fibres

a muscle fibre

fast twitch (white)

Movement production and control ●●●

The muscular system allows us to maintain our body position and move body parts. The body's nervous system enables us to coordinate and control our movements. The nervous system consists of the brain, spinal cord, nerve fibre and effector and receptor organs. Nerve cells or neurones carry the information to and from the spinal cord and brain; sensory neurons receive information from the receptor organs and transmit impulses to the brain, where the information is processed, then motor neurons transmit impulses from the brain to the effector organs such as the muscles.

Neurones have two main sections. Dentrites receive impulses from other nerve cells. These impulses are then transmitted along the axon. At the end of the axon the impulses divide into branches which form synapses with other neurons. Neurones are not actually connected to each other but are separated by tiny gaps known as synapses.

Impulses are able to cross this gap via the release of a chemical substance called acetylcholine, which allows an impulse to travel through the nervous system at great speed.

Within a muscle one motor neurone will stimulate a number of muscle fibres (up to 2000 fibres). Generally, small muscles capable of precise movements are composed of motor units with few muscle fibres, whereas muscles that create large or gross movements contain motor units with a large number of muscle fibres. Each motor unit obeys the all-or-none law: all the fibres in a single motor unit receive the same neural stimulation, so they all act maximally when the threshold of stimulation is met.

The force exerted by a muscle is dependent on the number of motor units recruited and the frequency of the stimulation, together this is referred to as the gradation of contraction. Generally the more units recruited and/or the greater the frequency of stimulation, the greater the tension developed by the muscle and the greater the force the muscle can apply.

Checkpoint 1

List the structures that make up the body's nervous system.

The jargon

Synapse – the main role of the synapse is to convey action potential between neurones.

Checkpoint 2

Explain what is meant by the all-or-none law.

The jargon

Together the *neurone* and the *fibres* it stimulates make up what is called the *motor unit*.

The jargon

All-or-none law: a neurone or muscle fibre either responds completely or not at all to a stimulus.

Checkpoint 3

What structures make up a motor unit?

Checkpoint 4

Explain the difference in function between effector organs and receptor organs.

Exam question   answers: page 14

Explain what is meant by the terms Type I, Type IIa and Type IIb muscle fibres and comment on their relevance to particular types of sporting activity.

(10 minutes)

The cardiovascular system

The cardiovascular system is made up of the heart (cardio) and the circulatory network of the blood vessels (vascular). These two systems work together to ensure that the body receives a constant supply of blood. The heart is responsible for pumping blood around the body, to the lungs for oxygenation and to the rest of the body (tissues, organs and cells) for all bodily functions. This process includes sending oxygenated blood to the muscles for exercise. If we carry out a sustained programme of aerobic exercise, the cardiovascular system adapts and makes this transport of blood more efficient. This is a popular area for examination questions and it is well worth spending time working through the spread making sure you understand all areas.

The heart

The heart is at the centre of the circulatory system, situated in the thorax between the lungs, it is a four-chambered pump as shown in the diagram below.

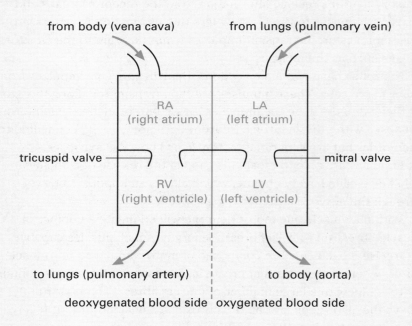

It consists largely of cardiac muscle, a specialised tissue that is capable of virtually unlimited rhythmical contraction and relaxation.

Blood flow

Deoxygenated blood enters the right side of the heart via the vena cava passing into the right atrium.

The right atrium contracts and forces the blood into the right ventricle through the tricuspid valves.

The ventricle then contracts; the same happens on the left-hand side since both sides of the heart contract simultaneously but the left ventricle wall is much thicker and greater force is generated when it

The jargon

The *tricuspid valve* has three flaps and prevents blood from flowing back into the right-hand side of the heart.

Checkpoint 1

Why is the left ventricle thicker walled than the right ventricle?

The jargon

Systole is a contraction phase of the cardiac cycle and *diastole* is the relaxation phase.

contracts, forcing blood initially into the aorta and then around the rest of the body.

The bicuspid valve prevents blood flowing back into the left-hand side of the heart.

Control of heart beat ●●●

The series of events that sees blood pass through the heart is referred to as the cardiac cycle.

The heart muscle is myogenic and does not need stimulation via the nervous system. The sinoatrial node (SAN) found in the right atrium acts as the heart's pacemaker. A wave of electrical stimulation arises from the SAN and then spreads over the two atria causing them to contract more or less at the same time. This stimulation reaches the atrioventricular node (AVN) found in the centre of the two atria, this channels the impulse along the Purkinje tissue found in the walls of the ventricles. This stimulation is followed by the simultaneous contraction of the ventricles.

Heart rate (HR) ●●●

The rate at which the heart beats and the volume of blood pumped out at each beat can be varied.

Cardiac output (Q) = Heart rate (HR) × Stroke volume (SV)

Venous return ●●●

The heart can only pump as much blood as it receives, any increase in cardiac output is dependent on the venous return increasing a similar amount of blood. During exercise the effects of the 'muscle pump' means that there is an increase in the amount of blood returning to the heart. This causes the walls of the heart to stretch more than normal. This over-stretching stimulates the SA node to increase the heart rate and there is also an increase in the force of contraction. This effect is known as Starling's Law, and explains the relationship between an increase in stroke volume and an increase in venous return.

Control of blood supply ●●●

Changes to the cardiac output are effected through the autonomic nervous system:

→ Impulses from the **parasympathetic fibres** slow down the heart beat.
→ Impulses from the **sympathetic fibres** accelerate it.

The cardiac centre of the brain controls the parasympathetic and sympathetic impulses.

When we take part in physical activity a number of changes occur in the cardiovascular system.

The jargon

Stroke volume is the volume of blood ejected from the heart in one beat, measured in ml/beat.

The jargon

Venous return is the volume of blood returning to the right atrium of the heart.

The jargon

The muscle pump is a term used to describe the increase in flow of blood back to the heart caused by the contracting of the skeletal muscles squeezing blood through the veins.

Checkpoint 2

What effect does stimulation of the parasympathetic system have on heart beat?

Checkpoint 3

What effect does stimulation of the sympathetic system have on heart beat?

Exam question   answer: page 14

Define venous return and explain how it is aided by exercise.   (6 minutes)

The role of blood in transporting oxygen

Our muscles require energy to contract to enable us to produce physical movement. There are energy supplies within the working muscles but these are used up very quickly. Therefore we need a method of transporting oxygen into the muscles. About 8 per cent of our body weight is made up of blood, this important element is the substance in which various essential materials such as oxygen are transported around the body.

Transporting oxygen

When we exercise, the body needs to take in and transport more oxygen. In the capillaries around the alveoli, oxygen combines with haemoglobin and is transported as oxyhaemoglyobin to the tissues where the oxygen dissociates, due to the diffusion gradient. Within muscles oxygen is transported by myoglobin to the mitochondria, where aerobic respiration takes place.

The effect of warming up and cooling down

A warm-up before strenuous physical activity has a direct effect on the cardiovascular system.

Vasodilation leads to

→ increase in oxygen flow to the muscles
→ increase in temperature
→ increase in enzyme activity
→ decrease in blood viscosity
→ oxygen dissociates from haemoglobin ore readily.

The purpose of a cool-down is to help the body return to its normal state as soon as possible. A thorough cool-down routine will help keep the blood flow high, washing out all the waste products the muscles have produced, preventing blood pooling and helping to replenish the fuel stores.

Blood pressure

Blood pressure is the pressure needed to pump blood around the body, the average BP reading for an adult (measure using a sphygmomanometer) is 120/80mmHg. The first number represents systolic pressure when the heart forcefully ejects blood. The second figure represents diastolic pressure when the heart relaxes. If a person's blood pressure is consistently above 140/90mmHg they are said to be suffering from hypertension and this can become a problem if left untreated. The heart has to work too hard and becomes inefficient, and this can commonly lead to a number of cardiovascular diseases including strokes and heart attacks. BP values can be affected by a number of factors such as age (arteries in older people are less elastic), stress and tension, diet and exercise.

The jargon

Diffusion gradient is the net movement of molecules of a fluid from a high concentration to a low concentration.

Checkpoint 1

Where does oxygen enter the body's blood network?

The jargon

Myoglobin combines with oxygen to form oxymyoglobin, it has greater affinity with oxygen than haemoglobin.

Checkpoint 2

Why does myoglobin transport oxygen within the muscles?

Checkpoint 3

Explain the term 'vasodilation' in reference to the cardiovascular system.

and carbon dioxide

The effects of exercise on blood

A sustained programme of continuous or aerobic training can result in an increase of up to 8 per cent in blood volume. The corresponding increase in red blood cells means that more oxygen can be transported around the body to the muscles. Another method of increasing the number of red blood cells in the body is to train at altitude. At high altitude the blood oxygen levels decrease, stimulating the body to produce more red blood cells.

The increased demand for oxygen in the working muscles causes an increase in heart rate, this is also helped by the release of the hormone adrenaline.

This increase in heart rate depends on how strenuous the activity is. The heart is able to pump more blood more quickly around the circulatory system. As more blood returns to the heart the cardiac muscle is stretched more than usual and this stimulates SAN to increase heart rate and it also increases the force of contraction, this is referred to as Starling's Law.

Blood flow is directed to the working muscles, heart and brain since they need more oxygen, whereas other areas of the body (the stomach and gut for example) do not require the oxygen as urgently. This process is known as vascular shunting. Blood distribution is also aided by precapillary sphincters, rings of muscle that surround blood vessels at the junction between an arteriole and capillary. It can effectively open and close the capillary and facilitates shunting.

Checkpoint 4

Describe the type of activities that should be included in a cool-down for a sport of your choice.

Exam questions   answers: page 14

The heart plays an essential role in allowing the body to take part in a wide range of physical activity.

1   Explain the short-term effect that exercise has on stroke volume, cardiac output and heart rate.   (6 minutes)

2   Describe the effect that physical exercise has on blood flow, blood velocity and blood pressure, accounting for any changes.   (7 minutes)

The respiratory system

Examiner's secrets

Though you will not be directly examined on this area it is useful to have a sound knowledge of the structure of the respiratory system.

Checkpoint 1

How is the trachea protected against closure?

Checkpoint 2

State two effects on breathing when taking exercise.

The human body needs a constant supply of oxygen, this oxygen is used to break down food to release energy. The body takes in oxygen continually from the air, as well as expelling carbon dioxide, a by-product from the breakdown of food into energy. This process of exchanging gases within the lungs is known as respiration.

The lungs

In order to get oxygen into our circulatory system, we first need to inhale air. This air ends up in our lungs, two spongy elastic bags in the airtight thoracic cavity, which extract oxygen from the inhaled air. Air is drawn into the lungs via the trachea. The lungs consist of a branching network of tubes called bronchioles (see diagram below). The bronchioles end in a small sac called alveoli and it is here that gaseous exchange takes place.

When we are resting, breathing is a process that occurs automatically. As we inhale, the only muscle that contracts is the diaphragm. This dome-shaped muscle flattens, increasing the volume of the thoracic cavity and causing air to rush into the lungs. As the diaphragm relaxes, it returns to its original shape, reducing the volume of the thoracic cavity and forcing air out of the lungs.

During exercise the demand for oxygen grows and we need to use extra muscles to help us breathe. The external intercostals aid inhalation, the internal intercostals aid exhalation.

Respiration at rest

When we breathe at rest we inhale and exhale between 12 and 16 times a minute. This is known as our respiratory rate. Each time we breathe, about 500ml of air is moved. This is called our tidal volume and it can be measured using a spirometer. The amount of air we breathe in one minute is known as minute ventilation and can be calculated by multiplying tidal volume and respiratory rate. Even after maximum expiration about 1.5 litres of air remains in the lungs. This is called the residual volume.

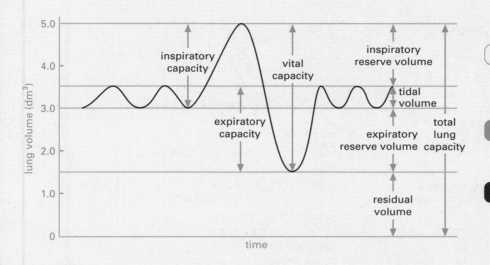

Action point

Study the graph and state the volumes of gas exchanged for each of the terms.

Checkpoint 3

What does a spirometer measure?

Examiner's secrets

Lung volumes is a popular focus for questions, take a calculator to the exam in case you have to work out volumes.

Checkpoint 4

What happens to residual volume during physical activity?

The jargon

Tidal volume is the amount of air moved each time we breathe, usually about 500ml.

Gaseous exchange   ●●●

In the alveoli there is a thin film of moisture in which the oxygen dissolves and then diffuses into blood capillaries. Carbon dioxide diffuses from the blood into the alveoli (see diagram below).

Control of breathing   ●●●

Breathing is controlled by a respiratory centre found within the medulla oblongata. The centre is sensitive to PH levels in the blood and also receives information from chemoreceptors around the body that can detect changes in PH levels, which is an indicator of changing carbon dioxide concentration.

Exam questions   answers: page 15

1   Describe the pathway taken by air travelling from the nostrils to the blood capillaries in the left lung.   (8 minutes)

2   How are the terminal structures of the lungs specialised for the process of gaseous exchange?   (6 minutes)

Answers
Anatomy and physiology

The skeletal and muscular system

Checkpoints

1 The characteristics of synovial joints that allow a great range of movement are: synovial joints have a fluid sac that lubricates the joints. The bones do not actually articulate, allowing a range of movement. The ends of the bones are covered with cartilage which act as a shock absorber.
2 The differing roles of ligaments and tendons are that: ligaments attach bone to bone and prevent unwanted movement, tendons attach muscle to bone and act as a pulley.
3 The functions of the human skeleton are:
   1 provides **shape**
   2 supports body in correct **posture**
   3 **supports** the internal organs
   4 **protects** the body
   5 sites of **muscle attachment**
   6 creates levers
   7 enables us to make **movements**
   8 **produces** blood cells.
4 The epimysium's role is to protect the muscle and help it slide smoothly past nearby muscles, bones and other organs as it changes in length.

Exam question

The functions of the skeleton facilitate physical activity by:
- providing shape for our bodies
- supporting body in correct posture
- supporting and protecting vital organs during movement
- providing a site for muscle attachment
- working as a lever system
- storing calcium, nutrients and minerals needed to repair after strenuous activity.

Motion and movement

Checkpoints

1 The structures that make up the body's nervous system consist of the brain, spinal cord, nerve fibre and effector and receptor organs.
2 The all-or-none law states that all the fibres in a single motor unit receive the same neural stimulation, so they all act maximally when the threshold of stimulation is met.
3 The neurone and muscle fibres it stimulates make up what is called the motor unit.
4 The difference in function between effector organs and receptor organs are:
   1 Effector organs receive information and instructions from the brain.
   2 Receptor organs transmit information to the brain.

Exam question

The terms Type 1, Type IIa and Type IIb muscle fibres mean:
Type 1 – slow oxidative fibres – endurance activities such as middle and long distance running, swimming and cycling.

Type 11a – Fast oxidative glygolytic fibres (FOG) – fast anaerobic activities such as sprinting.
Type 11b – Fast oxidative fibres (FG) – speed and power, in short bursts, for example in weightlifting.

The cardiovascular system

Checkpoints

The left ventricle is thicker walled than the right ventricle because:
1 The left ventricle pumps blood around the whole body, whereas the right ventricle only pumps blood from the heart to the lungs.
2 The effect that parasympathetic system has on the heart beat is that it slows down the heart.
3 Stimulation of the sympathetic system speeds up the heart.

Exam question

Venous return is the volume of blood returned to the right atrium. It is aided by exercise in that the muscle pump action forces more blood back to the heart. Exercise will also cause hypertrophy of the heart creating a more forceful pump.

The role of blood in transporting oxygen and carbon dioxide

Checkpoints

1 Oxygen, via the blood, enters the blood network via the alveoli within the lungs.
2 Myoglobin transports oxygen within the muscles because it has a greater affinity with oxygen than haemoglobin.
3 Vasodilation in reference to the cardiovascular system is where the diameter of a blood vessel increases as the surrounding muscles relax, this cause an increase in blood flow.
4 A cool-down should include light continuous exercise that maintains a higher than normal heart rate and also stretching.

Exam questions

1 Short-term effect of exercise on:
   Stroke volume – increases
   Heart rate – increases
   Cardiac output – increases
2 Effects of physical exercise on blood:
   Blood flow – increases due to the increased needs of the muscles; shunting means blood is moved away from some areas; muscles need lots of blood and oxygen
   Blood velocity – increases, since the heart needs to pump harder and faster; may depend on type of blood vessel
   Blood pressure – increases due to increased heart rate; many blood vessels may also undergo vasoconstriction which also increases pressure.

The respiratory system

Checkpoints

1 The trachea is protected against closure by rings of cartilage.
2 Two effects on breathing when taking exercise are that there is an increase in the depth and frequency of breathing.
3 A spirometer records the depth and frequency of breathing and can be used to study oxygen consumption.
4 Residual volume stays the same during physical activity.

Exam questions

1 The pathway of air when travelling from the nostrils to the blood capillaries in the left lung is as follows:

pharynx → larynx → trachea → left bronchus → left bronchiole → alveolus.
2 The terminal structures of the lungs are specialised for the process of gaseous exchange by: vast surface area, very thin walled/one cell thick, elastic tissue, moist membrane, extensive surrounding blood supply, extensive capillary network.

Revision checklist
Anatomy and physiology

1	Describe the structure and function of the skeletal system	Confident	Not confident. **Revise** pages 4–5
2	Describe and discuss the types of movement that can occur in the main synovial joints of the body	Confident	Not confident. **Revise** pages 4–5
3	Give an overview of the structure of muscles and their role in creating movement	Confident	Not confident. **Revise** pages 4–7
4	Describe how skeletal muscle is divided into three main fibre types	Confident	Not confident. **Revise** pages 5–7
5	Explain how the muscular system allows us to maintain our body position and move body parts	Confident	Not confident. **Revise** pages 5–7
6	Understand how the body's nervous system enables us to coordinate and control our movements	Confident	Not confident. **Revise** pages 5–7
7	Describe the structure and function of the heart	Confident	Not confident. **Revise** pages 8–9
8	Understand how blood supply is controlled	Confident	Not confident. **Revise** pages 8–9
9	Describe how the body transports oxygen around the body	Confident	Not confident. **Revise** pages 8–11
10	Explain the effects of warming up and cooling down	Confident	Not confident. **Revise** page 10
11	Understand the effects of exercise on blood	Confident	Not confident. **Revise** pages 10–11
12	Describe the mechanics of respiration	Confident	Not confident. **Revise** pages 12–13
13	Understand how breathing is controlled by a respiratory centre in the brain	Confident	Not confident. **Revise** pages 12–13

Skill acquisition

Skill is defined as the learnt ability to bring about pre-determined results with maximum certainty with the minimum outlay of energy. Skilled performers show the consistent characteristics of efficiency, coordination, fluency and a high level of technique. We will revise the different types of skills, their characteristics and the varied continua used in an attempt to classify skills. Performing well in sport relies on inherited abilities and we will look at the key characteristics of ability. The way that we gather information, decide what needs to be done and then execute a response is referred to as information processing. Once learnt, skills are retained in the memory and we need to understand the memory process and also suggest strategies for improving our retention and retrieval of information. Performance in competition is affected by our motivation and level of arousal and this may depend on the stage of learning we are in. How we learn skills is also affected by the quality of guidance and demonstration we are given.

Exam themes

→ Characteristics of skilled performance

→ The classification of sports skills

→ Skills, ability and information processing

→ Information processing and memory

→ Motor and executive programmes

→ Memory and learning theories

→ Motivation, guidance and improving performance

→ The role of reinforcement and demonstration in the learning of skills

→ Guidance and teaching styles

Topic checklist

AS ○   A2 ●

	AQA	EDEXCEL	OCR	WJEC
Characteristics and types of skills	○	Not examined	○	○
Memory	○		○	○
Motivation	●		○	●
Feedback	○		○	○

Characteristics and types of skills

Skill is the learnt ability to bring about pre-determined results with maximum efficiency, often with the minimum outlay of time or energy or both.

Knapp

Skilled performance is said to be:

→ intentional and consistent
→ goal directed
→ learnt – practice is required
→ high quality
→ minimum energy outlay
→ maximum efficiency.

Perceptual, cognitive and motor skills

→ **Perceptual skill** – complex definition – involves interpretation of stimuli – based on demands and past experiences.
→ **Cognitive skill** – skill in mental processes such as learning.
→ **Motor skill** – task that has a goal and requires body and/or limb movement.

Ability

Ability is seen as **innate** (genetically determined) and enduring, often enhanced by early childhood experience.

Ability allows us to complete various tasks, although there are actually two identified types of ability:

Psychomotor ability involves the *processing* of information and the *initiation* of movement
and
gross motor ability involves *actual movement* of the body.

Classifying movement skills

This is where we place and justify movement skills on a variety of continua, the most common are:

→ **Muscular involvement** which ranges from gross (large) to fine (delicate).
→ **Environmental influence** which ranges from open (unpredictable and changing) to closed (stable and predictable).
→ **Continuity** which ranges from discrete (definite start and end), serial (linked series of sub routines) and continuous (no clear beginning or end).
→ **Pacing** ranging from externally paced to internally paced.
→ **Difficulty** ranging from simple to complex.
→ **Organisation** ranging from low to high.

Information processing

This is the process where the sports performer gathers information, decides an what action is required and then reacts accordingly, in sport this all has to happen in a split second (see diagram).

Checkpoint 1

Explain the main difference between a skill and an ability.

Checkpoint 2

Why do we try and classify skills?

Feedback is received from both internal and external sources and means that the performer can make adjustments if the same situation arises again.

Schmidt identified three basic phases to information processing:

→ **Stage 1 stimulus identification** Here the sense organs of the body pick up information from the environment looking for cues.
→ **Stage 2 response selection** Once all the information has been received a decision is made.
→ **Stage 3 response programming** The decision taken sets in motion an appropriate response, this will often be a motor programme.

Motor programmes ●●●

Also referred to as '**executive programmes**', stored movement patterns held in the long-term memory that can be retrieved when a certain stimulus is received.

The speed that we process this information and elicit a response is known as **reaction time**, the time between starting and finishing the movement is called **movement time**. The time between the stimulus being identified and the completion of the movement is referred to as the **response time** and can also be calculated by using reaction time plus movement time.

There are several factors that affect these times:

→ Whether the reaction requires choice.
→ Age and sex of performer.
→ Whether the performer is expecting a stimulus also known as stimulus–response compatibility.
→ Previous experience.
→ How quickly one response follows the other, known as the psychological refractory period.
→ Anticipation of what is going to happen.

The single-channel hypothesis states that we can only deal with one stimulus at a time, this is how sports performers can 'sell a dummy', if we can get our opponent to wrongly anticipate our action it takes too long for them to change their decision if we then alter our move.

Examiner's secrets

Other versions of the diagram may be given in the exam paper, don't worry just work through each stage, looking for the three basics phases.

Checkpoint 3

Can you describe the three phases of the information-processing model.

Examiner's secrets

A theory linked to the psychological refractory period is the single-channel hypothesis and this is often the focus for questions.

Checkpoint 4

Explain the link between 'selling a dummy' in sport and the single-channel hypothesis.

Exam question   answer: page 26

Explain how a tennis serve contains both open and closed elements.

(6 minutes)

Memory

Memory plays a very important part in how performers process information. Previous experiences affect how we interpret the information we receive when playing sport. Often our previous experiences in sport can affect how we judge and interpret information when we perform.

Types of memory ●●●

Memory is a complex concept although the basic aspects can be summarised in the following diagram:

Short-term sensory store (STSS) – large capacity but can only hold information for up to one second, acts as a filter leading to selective attention.

Short-term memory – often referred to as the 'working memory', decides what needs to be done, limited capacity 7+/–2 items for about 30 seconds, information that is considered important or that can be rehearsed is passed on to the long-term memory store.

Long-term memory – has limitless capacity and can hold information for long periods of time. Memory that passes in to the LTM will have been encoded (chunked or association); motor programmes are stored in the LTM since they can be rehearsed.

Strategies to help improve information retention and retrieval include chunking, repetition or rehearsal and association.

Learning theories ●●●

There are two main schools of thought.

Associationist/connectionist	Cognitive
Stimulus – Response S–R	Intervening variables
Conditioned by stimuli – connected to response	Thinking leading to insight learning
Classical – Pavlov – conditioned reflex	Insight is facilitated by past experiences
Operant – Skinner – trial and error	Gestaltists – whole (Koffka, Koehler)
Drive theory – Hull	Leads to whole practice

The jargon

Selective attention is where the STSS sorts out relevant and irrelevant information allowing the sports performer to concentrate on the important information and shut out any distractions.

Checkpoint 1

Describe the three types of memory we use.

Checkpoint 2

Explain how the strategy of chunking helps us to retain and retrieve information.

The jargon

Chunking – where different pieces of information can be grouped or chunked together making it easier to remember as one piece of information.

Checkpoint 3

Explain the difference between the cognitive and associationist theories of learning.

The jargon

Insight learning means using memory to help solve problems.

Phases of learning

Fitts and Possner identified three phases of learning:

Phase	Description
Cognitive phase	Beginners phase, lots of trial and error, lots of positive feedback required
Associative phase	Motor or intermediate phase, associates movement with mental image, motor programme developing
Autonomous phase	Automatic, little conscious thought, distractions ignored, motor programmes now in LTM

Transfer

Refers to the influence of the learning or performance of one skill on the learning or performance of another. There are a number of different types of transfer we investigate in sports:

Type of transfer	Description
Positive	Where a skill can help with the learning of another
Negative	Where a skill hinders the learning of another
Proactive	Influences a skill yet to be learnt
Retroactive	Influences the performance of a previously learnt skill
Bilateral	Transfer of skill learnt on one side of body to the other side

Schmidt's schema theory is similar to the theory of transfer, skills learnt in one sport can be used in others as the performer has developed a general set of motor programmes that helps skills to be adapted to suit the sporting situation. This also solves the problem of having to store millions of separate motor programmes for every conceivable sporting movement.

Checkpoint 4

Which of Fitts and Possner's phases of learning do we usually associate with beginners?

Examiner's secrets

You need to know the characteristics for each of the phases of learning and be able to give practical examples of how this knowledge would be used in improving a performer's skill level.

Action point

Give a practical example from sport for each of the types of transfer highlighted in the table.

The jargon

A *schema* is a mental framework or outline developed through past experience.

Exam question   answer: page 26

Schmidt introduced the concept of 'schema theory'. Using the practical example of a basketball shot, explain the components of this theory.

(6 minutes)

Motivation

To be able to perform at our best in sport, we have to *want* to perform well and achieve. This drive to do well is referred to as motivation, the job of the coach or captain in sport is to motivate their teams to perform at their very best.

Types of motivation in sport

Motivation is the need and desire to perform at our best. There are two main factors that can affect motivation: extrinsic and intrinsic.

Intrinsic motivation	Extrinsic motivation
Internal drive to perform well	Rewards such as medals, money, prizes
Positive emotions	Significant others may also motivate
Martens – mastery of task and self-achievement	Rewards act as reinforcers

Demonstration and presentation of skills

→ Demonstrations are very important in learning sports skills and this links to the theories of observational learning and guidance.
→ Practice sessions should include activities that allow for the maximum amount of transfer to take place.

Part practice and whole practice

The teaching of skills in practice sessions often varies depending on the skills being taught, complex routines in sports like gymnastics are best taught by breaking them up into smaller parts called sub routines, this type of practice is called part practice.

Where the skill is more dynamic or continuous such as a golf swing or a tennis serve it is better to teach the whole skill to allow the learner to get the true feel for the skill, this is called whole practice.

Other methods of teaching include progressive part where the learner learns one part of the skill before moving on to learn the next sub routine, this is often referred to as 'linking'.

The whole part whole method is a combination of the whole and part methods, the whole skill is taught first to give the learner experience of the whole skill and it is broken down to refine the individual sub routines.

The concept of transfer

Transfer refers to the influence of the learning or performance of one skill on the learning or performance of another. This influence can be positive where it helps the new skill or it can be negative where it hinders the learning or performance of the other skill.

Don't forget

Motivation is the internal mechanisms and external stimuli which arouse and direct our behaviour.

Checkpoint 1

Explain the difference between intrinsic and extrinsic motivation.

The jargon

Significant other is a person who a performer relates to and holds in high esteem.

Links

Check out how motivation is linked to arousal levels in the sports psychology section.

Proactive transfer is where the influence is on a skill yet to be learnt, whereas retroactive transfer is where the influence is on the performance of a previously learnt skill.

There are three main types of **guidance** that are used in teaching skills in sport:

Type of guidance	Description
Visual	Showing what needs to be done either by demonstration or using video
Verbal	Telling the performer what needs to be done
Physical	Manually or mechanically assisting the performer to carry out the task

Teaching styles ●●●

Mosston and Ashworth identified a variety of teaching styles:

Teaching style	Description
Command	Teacher makes all the decisions
Reciprocal	Learners work in pairs, become teachers
Discovery	Decisions made by learner with guidance/ input from teacher
Problem solving	Learner makes all the decisions

Successful teachers and coaches tend to adopt a range of the above styles depending on the conditions and in order to respond to the needs of their pupils.

Checkpoint 2

What type of sports skills is best taught using the part practice model?

The jargon

Physical guidance helps to develop *kinaesthetic awareness*, this is where the performer has an awareness of body and limb position during movement.

Checkpoint 3

Give an example where manual guidance can help a performer cope with fear.

Checkpoint 4

What variables should be taken into account when choosing a teaching style?

Exam questions   answers: page 26

Motivation is a key element in preparing for a sports performance.

1   Explain the term 'intrinsic motivation'.   (4 minutes)

2   What external pressures can affect the motivation of a performer preparing for a high-level sports competition?   (8 minutes)

Examiner's secrets

You will need to be able to justify the effective use and limitation for each style of teaching.

Feedback

Feedback is the process which tells us how we are getting on while we perform a skill and afterwards can tell us how well we did. Feedback also completes the loop of the information-processing system, becoming part of the input and so affecting the performer's next decision (see diagram).

Types of feedback ●●●

There are several forms of feedback:

Type	Description
Continuous feedback	Feedback during the performance, often in the form of kinaesthesis.
Terminal feedback	Feedback after the skill has been executed
Knowledge of results	A type of terminal feedback that gives the performer information about the end result
Knowledge of performance	Information on how well the skill or movement is being performed
Internal or intrinsic feedback	A type of continuous feedback that reports how we feel, called proprioception
External or extrinsic feedback	Feedback that comes from an external source such as a coach
Positive feedback	Feedback that reinforces the learning or performance of a skill or gives information about a successful outcome
Negative feedback	Feedback on an unsuccessful result, can be used to prepare for future performance

In practice feedback in sport is usually divided into two methods: knowledge of performance and knowledge of results. Both types can be used to help motivate a performer, however, if used incorrectly they can hinder future performance.

Knowledge of performance ●●●

Knowledge of performance tells the performer how well or badly they are performing/executing a skill. Some of this feedback comes from proprioception, this is our own body awareness, you can feel how hard you have struck a ball in football or hit the ball in a golf shot. Knowledge of performance can also be given as an external source of feedback from a coach or peer, they can give verbal feedback on your performance.

Checkpoint 1

Explain the difference between external feedback and internal feedback.

The jargon

Proprioception is the awareness of the shape and position of the body, an internal form of feedback.

Videoing particular elements of a performance and then analysing the execution of skill can also be an effective form of this feedback.

Knowledge of results ●●●

Knowledge of results gives a performer feedback on the outcome of their actions. Once again it can come from a number of different sources, in some sports such as gymnastics proprioception can give the performers feedback on the outcome, they can feel that they have landed badly. Most, though, comes from external sources: a coach or teacher commenting on the performance. It is extremely important for the performer to know what the result of their action has been, there can be very little learning without knowledge of results especially in the early stages of learning a skill.

Both of these types of feedback play an important role in the concept of reinforcement. If a performance has been successful, either in terms of executing the skill or the result is good, then the performer will feel satisfied and the Stimulus–Response (S–R) bond is strengthened. Also understanding and feeling that the movement and result is good will help the performer form a picture of what is correct and to associate future performance with that model.

The importance of feedback when learning a new skill ●●●

→ Positive feedback that encourages the learner will motivate them to try harder.
→ Being told a performance was good by an external source helps to reinforce the skill in the performer's mind.
→ Feedback that gives suggestions on how to improve performance should result in more skilful movement.

The principles of feedback ●●●

The type of feedback given should depend on a number of factors:

→ The ability of the performer.
→ The type of activity being undertaken.
→ Personality of the performer.
→ Feedback needs to be given as soon as possible after the performance, the longer the delay between performance and feedback the less effective the feedback will be. The aim is to get the performers to associate the feeling of the skill with a positive result.
→ Any feedback given needs to be clear, concise and easily understood.

Exam questions answers: pages 26–27

Feedback involves using information that is available to a performer during and after the execution of a skill.

1 Outline the different types of feedback that can be used to help performers improve their performance.   (8 minutes)

2 What factors should a coach take into consideration before using feedback to help a performer improve?   (6 minutes)

Checkpoint 2

Explain the difference between knowledge of results and knowledge of performance.

Checkpoint 3

Explain the relationship between feedback and reinforcement.

Examiner's secrets

You will often be asked to give practical examples in your answer to questions on feedback, try and note down examples from your own sport where the various types of feedback could be used.

Checkpoint 4

What considerations should a coach take before deciding on the type of feedback to use with a performer?

Answers
Skill acquisition

Characteristics and types of skills

Checkpoints

1 The difference between a skill and an ability in that a skill is learnt, an ability is innate.
2 There are many different skills linked to such a variety of sporting activities that classification is an attempt to simplify the study of skills.
3 The three basic phases of information processing are:
Stage 1   stimulus identification
Stage 2   response selection
Stage 3   response programming.
4 The single-channel hypothesis states that we can only deal with one stimulus at a time, this is how sports performers can 'sell a dummy', if we can get our opponent to wrongly anticipate our action it takes too long for them to change their decision if we then alter our move.

Exam question

A tennis serve contains both open and closed skills.
Closed – isolated skill, not greatly affected by environment, movement replication always the same.
Open – factors such as heat and humidity can affect ball flight, server may perceive some movement of opponent and respond by changing their own movement, player can vary the type of serve.

Memory

Checkpoints

The three types of memory are:
1 Short-Term Sensory Store – large capacity but can only hold information for up to one second, acts as a filter leading to selective attention.
Short-term memory – often referred to as the 'working memory', decides what needs to be done, limited capacity 7+/–2 items for about 30 seconds.
Long-term memory – limitless capacity and can hold information for long periods of time.
2 The strategy of chunking helps us to retain and retrieve information by grouping units of information together into short phrases.
3 The difference between the cognitive and associationist theories of learning are: cognitive theories of learning suggest we need to understand a problem and learning is facilitated by past experiences and we then select an appropriate response. Associationist theories of learning suggest that we learn a specific response to a specific stimulus.
4 Beginners are usually associated with Fitts and Possner's cognitive phase.

Exam question

Experienced basketball player will have stored a program for the shot in their LTM. Recall scheme will start off the programme when the player wants to shoot. Adjustments may be made depending on external factors, after shot recognition schema – did it feel right, response outcome – was it successful?

Motivation

Checkpoints

1 Intrinsic motivation is an internal drive to perform well, extrinsic motivation includes rewards such as medals, money or prizes.
2 Complex routines in sports like gymnastics are best taught by breaking them up into smaller parts called sub routines.
3 An example of where manual guidance can help a performer cope with fear in by wearing arm bands in swimming.
4 Variables include the type and difficulty of the activity, the ability levels of the learners, the group's level of motivation, age of the learners and the environmental conditions.

Exam questions

1 Intrinsic motivation comes from an internal feeling/playing for its own sake, may include elements of fun, enjoyment and satisfaction, achieving a personal best or self-set goals. Would include achieving intrinsic rewards.
2 External pressures on a performer preparing for competition would include the following: external rewards that victory would bring, peer pressure from team, pressure from significant others (coach/manager/parents), pressure from opponents or previous experience, the importance of the task, presence of a large audience or media, the conditions or environment of the scheduled playing time.

Feedback

Checkpoints

1 Internal feedback is a type of continuous feedback that reports how we feel, called proprioception, whereas external feedback is feedback that comes from an external source such as a coach.
2 Knowledge of results gives a performer feedback on the outcome of their actions. Knowledge of performance tells the performer how well or badly they are performing/executing a skill.
3 Feedback on a successful performance will mean that the performer will feel satisfied and the S-R bond is strengthened. They will be more likely to be successful the next time they perform.
4 A coach should consider the following factors before deciding on the type of feedback:
   • the ability of the performer
   • the type of activity being undertaken
   • the personality of the performer.

Exam questions

The different types of feedback that can be used to help performs improve their performance are:

1 Continuous feedback available during performance. Terminal feedback, knowledge of results available after performance. Knowledge of performance, could be internal or intrinsic or external feedback from a coach giving verbal or visual guidance, positive feedback is used to reinforce learning.

2 Factors affecting the type of feedback used include the ability of the performer, what stage of learning they are in, the type and difficulty of activity, the personality of performer and the type of teaching style being used.

Examiner's secrets

Try and back up the points you make in answers with a named theory or the name of a scientist who has carried out research in that specific area.

Examiner's secrets

Very often a diagram can help you explain a difficult concept such as information processing in a more efficient way.

Revision checklist
Skill aquisition

By the end of this chapter you should be able to:

1	Define the characteristics and types of skills	Confident	Not confident. **Revise** pages 18–19
2	Explain the information processing model	Confident	Not confident. **Revise** pages 18–19
3	Discuss the different types of memory and the role they play in learning and producing sports skills	Confident	Not confident. **Revise** pages 20–21
4	Understand the theory and the practical application of motor programmes	Confident	Not confident. **Revise** pages 20–21
5	Describe the different types of motivation and their effects on sports performance	Confident	Not confident. **Revise** pages 22–23
6	Explain effective demonstration and presentation of skills to learners in sport	Confident	Not confident. **Revise** pages 22–23
7	Discuss the concept of transfer and its influence on the learning of skills	Confident	Not confident. **Revise** pages 22–23
8	Discuss the three main types that are used in teaching skills in sport	Confident	Not confident. **Revise** pages 22–23
9	Discuss how different teaching styles suit specific sporting situations	Confident	Not confident. **Revise** pages 22–23
10	Explain the role feedback plays in the learning of skills	Confident	Not confident. **Revise** pages 24–25
11	Give examples of the various types of feedback	Confident	Not confident. **Revise** pages 24–25
12	Discuss and give practical applications of the principles of feedback	Confident	Not confident. **Revise** pages 24–25

The social contemporary study of sport

The contemporary issues unit investigates how society can affect the sports performer and how society can be influenced by physical education and sport. The terms we use when describing the activities related to sport are technical, which can lead to confusion, so we need to review the key concepts and terms used in the sociological study of sport. You need to be able to analyse these different terms in order to develop a better understanding of why people get involved in physical education and sport at different levels and the factors which influence and restrict their choices. In some of the exam specifications this unit compares physical education and sport in the UK with that of other countries so that we can learn from the experiences of other cultures. Many social issues surround physical education and sport and we need to take an in-depth look at the main issues affecting the performer. Discrimination of all forms is unfortunately a feature of our society, in sport as in other aspects.

Exam themes

→ The concepts of sport, leisure, play and recreation

→ Physical and outdoor education in UK schools

→ Sport within different cultures around the globe

→ Sport in advanced cultures

→ The support and nurture of élite sport

→ Ethics and values in high-level sport

→ The concept of mass participation

→ Factors that affects a person's access to sport and recreation

→ Issues in the Olympic Games

Topic checklist

AS ○ A2 ●	AQA	EDEXCEL	OCR	WJEC
Sport, leisure and recreation: key concepts	○	○	○	○
Sport and culture			○	
Sport in advanced societies		●	○	●
Élite sport	●	○	○	○
Ethics and values in high-level sport	●	○●	○●	○
Sport and mass participation	○	○●	○	○●
Factors affecting participation	○	○	○	○●
The Olympic Games	○	○	○	●
Issues at the Olympics	○	○	○	●

Sport, leisure and recreation: key concepts

The study of sports sociology identifies the effect society can have on the sports performer and also the effect sport may have on society. We first need to review the different terms used to describe the sociological aspects of sport and physical education.

The key concepts ●●●

Sports have the following characteristics:

→ they all contain an element of **chance**
→ they all involve **competition** between **distinct sides**
→ **physically strenuous activity** is involved
→ the **clear outcome** has **winners** and **losers**
→ games are **spontaneous** and **enjoyable**
→ **special equipment** is usually needed to play.

Leisure ●●●

Key words for leisure: free time, choice, not work. Definitions of leisure tend to infer that it is time not at work, but work can include many things. Although there has always been some form of leisure throughout history, we all have more leisure time and can choose from a greater list of activities than people in the past.

Recreation ●●●

Physical recreation

Physical recreation is physical activity of a relaxing nature, with limited outcome and organisation. It is a positive use of leisure time, involving an activity worth doing. Physical recreation has a strong link with middle-class moral guidance of the nineteenth century. Intrinsic rewards dominate in physical recreation.

Outdoor recreation

Outdoor recreation involves challenging activities in the natural environment. Most people in Britain partake frequently in some form of outdoor recreation. For most people, the essential element is an escape from the urban environment. The most popular outdoor recreations are walking and fishing.

Play

Children play to increase their mastery of reality. Adults play to escape from reality. Because of its non-serious quality a number of dimensions of play can be identified:

→ Play must be freely undertaken. If constrained it is less playful.
→ Play is non-instrumental. It is an end in itself, you do not play for an outcome.

Take note

The key to leisure time is that you perform the activities that you *choose* to do.

Checkpoint 1

List four labour-saving devices that have enabled people who do housework to have more leisure time.

Checkpoint 2

Why, for professional sports performers, is a definition of leisure difficult?

Checkpoint 3

What factors have led to an increase in participation of outdoor sports?

→ Play generally has its own set of rules and regulations. It is very informal and any rules will be agreed by the participants and may well change during the activity.
→ Play activities involve uncertainty. Play is open-ended and has no limits.

Physical and outdoor education

In the UK, physical education takes place only in educational institutions (schools, colleges and universities). It always involves a 'teacher' passing on knowledge to a group of 'pupils' and is almost always concerned with bodily movement. However, it is a wide concept with many different interpretations. Even with the National Curriculum for physical education, no one school's programme is the same as another's. In recent years the academic study of physical education has grown greatly and it is now studied at many levels. The National Curriculum identifies six sport activity areas: games, athletics, gymnastics, dance, swimming and adventure. Schools should offer pupils experience in at least five of the activity areas.

Recent initiatives in physical education and school sport include TOP programmes, sport college status and the development of school sport coordinator networks.

Outdoor education

Outdoor education forms some part of most school curricula and is now a stated aim of the National Curriculum. However, in most schools it is only an extracurricular activity. The problems are that outdoor pursuits are very expensive in terms of transport and equipment needed, and many safety precautions must be considered, especially in the light of several recent tragedies.

The jargon

The *National Curriculum* is issued by the government, this sets out what schools should teach pupils, including physical education.

Examiner's secrets

You will often be asked to give examples of schemes and programmes used in schools to promote participation among schoolchildren as well as national programmes such as TOPs. You can also use local examples.

Checkpoint 4

What advantages might outdoor education have over normal lessons in the inculcation of social skills?

Exam question   answer: page 48

Explain the main differences between an activity that is a sport and one that is physical education.   (6 minutes)

Sport and culture

Sport is a reflection of society and many issues (such as class, gender and race) have an effect on sport. Sport follows the trends of society and a number of patterns can be identified.

Culture

Culture is the way the society functions and its traditions and beliefs.

Tribal societies

These are isolated groups of people who live in areas of the world that have not witnessed an industrial or urban revolution.

Examples include the Samoan, Aboriginal and Eskimo cultures.

Characteristics	
Natural	Use what can be found around them
Functional	Activities help to practise skills
Ritual	Linked to worship and religion
Ceremonial	Used to reinforce cultural values of tribe
Survival	Practising hunting and defence skills
Community	Used to select leaders or as initiatation in adulthood

Analysis of effects of

→ **Colonialism** – where many were forced to reject their traditional sports and take up colonial games, often Anglicised versions of cricket and rugby.
→ **Post-colonialism** – on regaining their independence many societies now combine traditions and customs with modern sport, epitomised by the Samoan 'Haka' in rugby.

Emergent cultures

These are the **developing countries**, such as the African nations. In these countries modern sport has often been introduced by previous colonial powers and in the main has replaced the indigenous activities. With their new-found independence, the people have used sport as a process of nation building.

The success of countries such as Kenya in athletics, the West Indies in cricket and Brazil in football has shown that developing countries can take on the developed world and often beat them.

These countries face the problems of limited resources and little infrastructure, but through selection and channelling in only a limited number of sports they are able to compete on the world stage. The model of sports development in these countries is shown in the table below.

Examiner's secrets

Try and investigate any links between your own sport and tribal societies.

Checkpoint 1

What is meant by the term 'colonialisation'?

Checkpoint 2

Explain the term 'nation building' with relation to sport.

An emergent model of sport

Integration	Sport unites the country by bringing together different races, areas and tribes
Defence	National Service gives a chance for selection. The strict regime is suited to training and development of talent
Shop window	Sporting success puts the country onto the world stage
Selection	Concentrate on a limited number of sports, usually the ones suited to the environment or the physique of the people

Many emergent countries have now introduced élite sports systems aimed at increasing the chance of gaining gold medals. Often the armed forces act as sports nurseries and screen for sports talent (Kenya is a good example of a country in which the army plays an important role in fostering sports talent).

Performers that do reach an élite level have the opportunity to earn a great deal of money and often move to Western countries, where the opportunity to gain higher reward is greater.

Ethnic sports ●●●

These are traditional events that are unique to a particular geographical or cultural area. Examples include the Highland Games in Scotland, various forms of mob football played throughout the UK, hurling in Cornwall and wrestling in Cumberland and Devon.

Characteristics	
Festival	Often annual events that are used to celebrate both religious and secular occasions
Local	Confined to a small geographical area, often as small as just one village or town
Traditional	Have been played for many years, involve local customs
Isolated	Areas are often in more rural areas, away from major conurbations

Reasons for the survival of many for these ethnic sports includes attracting tourism to areas and also a desire by local communities to retain elements of their ethnic identity.

Checkpoint 3

How can the armed forces in emergent cultures play a role in nurturing sports science?

Checkpoint 4

Define the term 'ethnic sport'.

Exam question   answer: page 48

How can sport be used for social mobility by emergent athletes?   (6 minutes)

Sport in advanced societies

Sport plays an important role in advanced societies, reflecting the wider values and traditions of the society. Most advanced cultures follow a capitalist economy, where private ownership dominates and the market drives most aspects of life including sport. Increasingly sport in advanced cultures is seen as a commodity, a chance for companies and individuals to make large amounts of money.

The American model ●●●

The sports are high scoring and action-packed to maximise their entertainment value. They reflect American culture in that the aim is to win – the win ethic is what drives all American people and this fuels the so-called 'American Dream'. But it is the commercial aspect of American sport which makes it so different. Every level, from professional national teams to the local high school football teams, is run as a business. The influence of television is total and most sports in the USA rely entirely on the money generated through television deals and advertising revenue. Sports stars in America are millionaires; most professional teams will have a number of players on multi-million-dollar annual contracts. Many stars, like Michael Jordan, make even more money through sponsorship deals and endorsements.

There is a flip side to this: sport in the USA is extremely élitist. In athletics, for example, there is not even one amateur club where 'Joe Public' can train. For most Americans, sport is something you watch on the television and not something you actually play. The television also dictates the rules; for example, American football has evolved into a constant stop–go staccato pattern to allow companies to screen advertisements every five minutes.

New World democratic cultures ●●●

Australia, South Africa and New Zealand. These are cultures with European origins and, in the main, former British colonies. Most are under 200 years old and, after achieving independence, developed into advanced thriving societies.

Checkpoint 1

Explain what is meant by the term 'American Dream'.

The jargon

Americanisation means where American trends and attitudes invade traditional culture. Many of these trends are beginning to filter into British sport, and it may be very difficult for us to prevent Americanisation of our sport.

Checkpoint 2

Give examples of how British sport is being Americanised.

What these countries have in common, apart from a shared colonial history, is a culture of 'Bush Ethos'. The environments remain harsh and the people have had to work hard to develop and expand. Being young countries they lack the traditions and history of the Old World and have consequently needed to find new ways of expressing their emotions. Sport has more than filled this role: it is often seen as a substitute for the higher forms of culture in Europe.

The other drive is again a form of shop window. The ambition of all these new cultures is to beat their old colonial powers – in particular England. Their sportsmen and women seem to have an extra edge to their approach, are driven by the win ethic and do not appear to be restrained by our more traditional values and ethics. To them, *winning* is important: it reflects struggle and hard work – the values that are inherent in their societies.

Checkpoint 3

Why do New World cultures tend to play sports that originated in the UK?

Checkpoint 4

Why has a country such as Australia placed so much emphasis on developing sports talent?

Exam question   answer: page 48

The dominant sporting ethic in advanced cultures is that winning is everything. Explain why this win ethic is so strong in modern advanced society.   (8 minutes)

Élite sport

Excellence in sport has two meanings: élitism, which means 'all for the best – forget the rest' or optimum performance, where everyone has the chance to succeed.

Most societies emphasise élitism as this produces champions, which can be used as a 'shop window'. There are three major stages in the development of excellence: selection, development and support. There is much diversity in the methods used by different societies.

An élite sports model

In élitism the emphasis is on a few, the best, performers. The tendency is to look for the most developed and to ignore the rest. We have already seen this approach in the emerging cultures discussed in the previous section. The best example of this approach was seen in the German Democratic Republic, a country with a population of only 16 million which managed to be in the top three for sports such as athletics, swimming and boxing. The whole sports system of this communist country was geared up to selecting and developing champion performers, but this was at the expense of the rest of the population.

The development of excellence

Three key stages may be identified in the development of sporting talent:

1 Selection of talent.
2 Development of talent.
3 Providing support for performance.

The actual methods used differ from country to country, but increasingly a number of policies are being followed by most. A lot of these have been adapted from the Eastern European model of sports excellence, pioneered by the Soviet Union and the German Democratic Republic from the 1950s onwards.

Selection

Selection is the start of this process, identifying individuals with the potential to become champions. The pyramid theory of sports development suggests that the wider the base then the greater the number at the top of the pyramid. The aim of the selection process is to make the base of the pyramid as wide as possible.

Talent development

Stage two is again a crucial aspect. The children selected are coached, instructed and nurtured to become champions. In many countries this process is achieved through the education system, predominantly in sports schools.

Checkpoint 1

Explain what is meant by the term 'shop window'.

Sports schools

Sports schools are found in most European countries and are often controlled by the state. They allow young people to develop their sporting potential while continuing with academic studies. They usually have high-quality facilities and specialised staff, the advantage being that students get more time to practise their skills and the atmosphere of excellence encourages their development.

Providing support for performance ●●●

The final part of the process is to provide support in terms of administration and funding. In many countries the state funds the top athletes – in Australia, France and the old Soviet Union all top performers are paid grants that allow them to become virtually full-time athletes. In America talented performers are paid scholarships by schools and colleges or athletes are contracted to a professional team. In the UK SportsAid tries to fund up-and-coming athletes – as yet there is little government input to sports in the UK.

Modern sports performers also require the support of an ever-increasing range of sports specialists (psychologists, dieticians, physiotherapists), as well as video and computer equipment to help improve technique. In the UK such a service is now being developed in a number of National Sports Centres forming a national network, with the United Kingdom Sports Institute (UKSI) as the central focus. The aim is to enable our international performers to use top-quality facilities for training. These now come under the Sports Council's World Class Performance programme, funded by the National Lottery. This Sports Fund has three levels:

→ **World Class Start** – programmes aimed at developing talented youngsters.
→ **World Class Potential** – assisting with the development of teenagers helping with educational support.
→ **World Class Performance** – supporting our élite athletes through financial support and providing top-class facilities through the UKSI.

The funding of UK Sport is prioritised to ensure the most effective use of lottery funds to achieve the overall aim of in the UK being in the world's top five sporting nations.

> **Checkpoint 2**
>
> List four advantages and four disadvantages of basing performers in sports schools.

> **Checkpoint 3**
>
> What is the role of the UKSI network?

> **Checkpoint 4**
>
> Describe the three stages in the development of sporting talent.

> **Exam question** answer: page 48
>
> To achieve excellence in sport, a high level of commitment, resources and expertise is necessary. Describe sporting agencies in the UK who are attempting to assist performers in achieving excellence. (10 minutes)

Ethics and values in high-level sport

Checkpoint 1

Define what is meant by the term 'deviance' in sport.

The jargon

Written rules are sometimes referred to as 'the spirit of the game', unwritten rules are values and ethics which we expect all sportsmen and women to follow.

Checkpoint 2

Give examples of the types of extrinsic rewards we can receive in sport.

The jargon

Sportsmanship means conforming to the written and unwritten rules of sport.

The jargon

Fair play means treating your opponent as an equal and abiding by the rules of your sport.

The jargon

Gamesmanship is where you use whatever means you can to overcome your opponent.

Checkpoint 3

Outline the main differences between sportsmanship and gamesmanship.

All sports have rules and deviance occurs when participants break these rules. We call this *cheating* and this is an important issue in modern sport.

Cheating is not a new concept – we know that the ancient Olympians took tonics to try to increase their performances. Some people would argue that cheating is an important element in sport and that without it sport would be dull.

Sport has many written rules but also *unwritten* rules, and these make investigation of deviance more complicated.

The concept of sportsmanship

Sport relies on **sportsmanship**, people conforming to the written and unwritten rules of sport. The idea of **fair play** means that you treat your opponent as an equal, and although you want to beat them, you will do so only by adhering to the rules and a code of conduct that has been developed in the sport through tradition. This includes shaking hands and cheering the other team off at the end of the game.

To cheat not only destroys the game but also detracts from your personal achievement. A win through cheating is a hollow victory as, although you may gain the extrinsic rewards, you will not gain the more fulfilling intrinsic ones.

Gamesmanship

The alternative dynamic in sport is known as **gamesmanship**, where you use whatever means you can to overcome your opponent. The only aim here is the win, and for most people it is not a question of breaking the rules – more bending them to your advantage.

Violence by spectators

So called hooliganism in sport is sadly not a new concept. Football is the sport usually associated with crowd disorder and there has been much research and debate about the reasons behind football hooliganism.

Some of the main reasons are:

→ Ritual importance of many football matches such as local derbies where other factors such as religion can be a contributing factor
→ Alcohol
→ Frustration at the result or poor decisions by officials
→ Pre-match hype in the media
→ Violence by players on the pitch
→ Poor stadia and ineffective methods of crowd control.

The problem has diminished in recent years, and the increased use of CCTV at football grounds and tighter controls on alcohol are generally seen as key factors in this.

Drugs in sport

Drug abuse has been one of the main areas of deviance in sport during the last few years. It is not clear whether the actual level of drug taking has gone up or whether we now know more about it because testing systems have improved. It is also very difficult to decide where the line should be drawn between illegal and legal substances – many athletes have tested positive but claim that all they took was a cough mixture or other such product which can be bought over the counter.

Drug taking is the ultimate in gamesmanship – taking something to increase your performance and increase your chances of winning.

Checkpoint 4

What is classed as a 'drug' in sport?

Exam question   answer: page 49

Sport relies on sportsmanship – people adhering to both the written and unwritten rules of the game they are playing. Explain what is meant by the terms written and unwritten rules in sport.   (10 minutes)

Sport and mass participation

Sport is a natural part of life, whether you are one of the élite competing for gold medals or just playing for fun and enjoyment. The opportunity to take part in sporting activity should be a basic human right; however, many people suffer constraints that prevent them from taking part. The aim of mass participation is to break down these constraints, whatever they may be, and to encourage as many people as possible to take up sport.

Checkpoint 1

What are the benefits of mass participation for *individuals*?

Take note

The Sports Council estimate that one in three people in the UK regularly take part in sport.

Checkpoint 2

What are the benefits of mass participation in sport for a *country*?

Checkpoint 3

From where did the concept of 'Sport for All' first emerge in the 1960s?

The Sports Council

The Sports Council has four main aims:

1 To increase participation in sport.
2 To increase the quality and quantity of sports facilities.
3 To raise standards of performance.
4 To provide information for and about sport.

In 1994 it was announced that the Sports Council would be reshaped to create two new bodies: the **UK Sports Council** and the **English Sports Council**, rebranded as **Sport England** in 1999. This brings England in line with the other home countries in that it now has its own Sports Council. The UK Sports Council has a coordinating role, ensuring that all councils work in the same direction, and has responsibility for drugs testing and doping control in all UK sport.

Each council is split further into regional and local sports councils, enabling area-specific planning. Funding for the Council comes from the National Lottery Sports Fund and Sport England receives £200 million per year. This money is used to run the regional councils, fund campaigns and capital projects and provide information services, although most of it is redistributed to sports governing bodies and institutions as grants to be used for increasing sports participation, building new facilities and setting up recreation programmes.

The 'Sport for All' campaign, originally set up in 1972 and still continuing, highlights the value of sport and that it is something to which all members of the community should have access. The campaign initially hoped to increase the opportunities for sport and recreation through developing more facilities, and by informing and educating the public on what was available. Recently the campaign has become more diverse by targeting groups of the community that remain under-represented in sport. Separate campaigns such as '50+ and All to Play For' (aimed at older people) and 'What's your Sport?' (aimed at women) have followed.

Sport for All in Europe

The concept of **Sport for All** first emerged in the early 1960s in Germany and the Nordic countries. In 1968, the **Council of Europe** initiated the setting up of several projects aimed at encouraging mass participation. Their stated aim was to:

Provide conditions to enable the widest possible range of the population to practise regularly either sport proper or various physical activities calling for an effort adapted to individual capacities.

Growing interest in sport and in the specific development of Sport for All by all European countries led to the adoption of the European Sport for All charter in 1972. This asserted that 'Every individual has the right to participate in sport' and that 'It is the duty of every member state to support financially and organisationally this ideal'.

The main organisation charged with implementing Sport for All has been the Committee for the Development of Sport (Comité Directeur pour le developpement du sport), known as the CDDS.

The performance pyramid ●●●

The different levels of sport can best be represented as a pyramid, and such a concept is used by many sports organisations in order to develop a continuum of participation from grass roots to élite. The broader the base of the participation then in theory the greater the élite pool a society can select from.

Performance pyramid

There are four levels of performance within the pyramid. The foundation level, also known as grass roots level, is mainly associated with young children being introduced to sport and learning the basic or fundamental motor skills. In the UK schemes such as TOP Sport and Dragon Sport have been used by the sports councils to promote participation at this level.

At the participation level older children are beginning to play full-scale sport, often for teams based in school or the community. The School Sport Co-ordinators programme and the Sport Education and Step into Sport initiatives are example of strategies used to encourage participation at this level.

The performance level is associated with participants who are committed to performing in formal organised competition at higher club and regional level. Participants will usually train for their chosen sport and are usually members of a local sport club or organisation.

The excellence level is where élite athletes perform at a national and/or international level. For many of these performers sport is their main focus or career; they receive funds either as a professional or through grants and awards from sports organsiations such as the Sports Lottery Fund.

The jargon

European Charter of Sport for All was set up in 1972, this aims to give every European individual the right to participate in sport.

Checkpoint 4

Name the four different levels of the performance pyramid.

Examiner's secrets

It may be easier to revise if you can use examples from the sport you play when referring to the different levels of the sports pyramid.

Exam question   answer: page 49

Participation in sport brings benefits for individuals and the community. Explain what some of these benefits may be.   (8 minutes)

Factors affecting participation

Many people do not have equal access to sport, often as a result of discrimination due to cultural variables. We can identify a number of so-called target groups in society, these are groups who consistently find it difficult to access sport and recreation.

Cultural factors

There are five main cultural factors that can lead to discrimination in sport:

→ gender
→ class
→ race
→ age
→ ability.

Discrimination can be said to affect the following areas in sport:

→ provision
→ opportunity
→ esteem.

Provision

Are the facilities that allow you to participate available to you? Living in an inner-city area would discriminate against you because there is little provision in these areas. Equipment is also required, which is often expensive – those on low incomes may be discriminated against unless equipment is available free or can be hired cheaply.

Opportunity

There may be barriers to an individual's participation in an activity. In the UK most sport takes place in the voluntarily run clubs, which are often élitist organisations. Clubs work on membership systems and membership is controlled either by the ability to pay the fees or, in cases such as some golf clubs, election to the club membership. This often closes membership to certain members of the community.

Another consideration for the individual is whether they have the time to play. Women in particular are often faced with this problem. The demands of work and family often mean that women have little leisure time, which accounts in some way for the low levels of female participation in sport.

Checkpoint 1

Explain the three factors that lead to discrimination in sport.

Checkpoint 2

Provision in sport relates to a person's access to what?

Checkpoint 3

How can a sports club act as a barrier to participation?

The jargon

Stereotypes are a group of characteristics that we believe all members of a certain section of society share, usually based on very little actual fact.

The jargon

Sports myths – stereotypes may lead to myths in sport, and this is where people are discriminated against. Common sports myths are that 'Black people can't swim' and that 'Women will damage themselves internally if they do the hurdles'. Again, myths are based on very little truth, but often become an important aspect in selection and opportunity.

Esteem

This is concerned with the societal view of individuals. In many cultures societal values dictate that women should not take an active part in sport, or if they do it should be confined to 'feminine' sports such as gymnastics and not 'macho' pursuits such as football or rugby. These judgements are based on the traditional roles men and women have taken in society and may be very difficult to break.

Stereotypes and **sports myths** are also societal variables that lead to discrimination. Often minority groups within a community are labelled as having certain characteristics or traits, and this can lead to them being steered into certain sports or positions and away from others.

One good example in the UK is the current lack of Asian footballers in soccer. Much research has been done into this area and programmes are now being set up to try to address the imbalance but the main problem is that, in our societal view, Asians are not potential footballers.

Stereotypes and myths can become 'self-fulfilling prophecies' – even the people they discriminate against come to believe they are valid and conform to the stereotypes by displaying their appointed characteristics and choosing the sports that fit them. In doing so they are reinforcing society's view. It is only recently that a number of women have broken this system by taking up football and rugby.

Checkpoint 4

Explain what is meant by the term 'self-fulfilling prophecies' in relation to sport.

Exam question   answer: page 49

Sport for all is not yet a reality in the UK. How can a person's opportunity to participate in sport be affected by socio-cultural factors?   (9 minutes)

The Olympic Games

The Olympic Games have their origins in Ancient Greece, where they were held every four years as part of a religious ceremony to the god Zeus. At the end of the last century Baron de Coubertin reintroduced the Games (the first being held in Greece in 1896), and set up the International Olympic Committee (IOC) and the modern Olympic Games, which are held every four years in a different city.

The modern games

There are actually two Olympic Games – winter and summer – though it is the summer Games that are the most prestigious. De Coubertin's idea was that the Games could be used to bring the people of the world together in friendly competition. He hoped that this might help prevent war and develop more international friendship.

The Olympics in the past have been used to promote the good side of sport. All competitors were amateurs, competing purely for enjoyment, and the winner's medal had no real monetary value. Sportsmanship was the central point of the Games, and before competition started all the athletes took the Olympic Oath.

The IOC organise each Games every four years, choosing the host city and coordinating funding. Most of the IOC's income now comes from selling the festoon (the five-rings symbol) to international companies and from television fees. Each participating nation must have a national Olympic body that takes responsibility for promoting the Olympic ideals in their own country. In the UK this is the British Olympic Association.

The British Olympic Association

This independent organisation is responsible for all Olympic matters in the UK, primarily entering competitors for the Olympic Games. Other functions include raising funds to enable British performers to compete at the Games and for the transportation, clothing and other expenses involved in sending a British team (up to £4 million). A more general role is to develop interest in the Olympic movement in Britain. It also helps to coordinate any bids to host the Games.

The jargon

The *International Olympic Committee*, the governing body of the Olympic movement.

Checkpoint 1

Explain the link between the Olympic Oath and the concept of sportsmanship.

The jargon

Olympic Oath: 'We swear that we will take part in these Olympic Games in the true spirit of sportsmanship and that we will abide by the rules that govern them, for the glory of sport and the honour of our country.'

The jargon

The festoon is the Olympic five-rings symbol, sold to the highest bidders among international companies.

The fund-raising role of the British Olympic Association is unique to the UK. In most other countries, even the USA, central government helps to finance the Olympic team – but the British Olympic Association raises all the money itself. This has traditionally been achieved through schoolchildren's sponsored events and donations from the general public and business. Increasingly, more money is being raised through commercial sponsorship, specifically in the use of the Olympic logo (you have probably seen the five-ring logo on Mars Bars and cans of Coca-Cola).

Drugs

Although the essence of the Olympics remains an amateur one, where the only reward winners receive is a token in the shape of an Olympic medal, the commercial opportunities now open to Olympians means that increasingly many are tempted to use illegal means to improve their performance.

The IOC has since 1967, when they set up the Olympic Medical Commission, taken the lead role in attempting to prevent the use of drugs in sport. Each year the IOC produces a list of banned drugs which it then tests for at the Games, most other sports governing bodies also use this list.

Checkpoint 2

What were de Coubertin's ideals behind the setting up of the modern Olympics?

Checkpoint 3

How does the IOC generate most of the funds it needs?

Take note

The 2004 Games were watched on TV by over four billion people worldwide.

Exam questions   answers: pages 49–50

1   What are the reasons for the increasing commercialisation of the Olympic Games?   (10 minutes)

2   *The goal of the Olympic movement is to contribute to building a peaceful and better world*. The Olympic Charter. Comment on the effectiveness of this claim.   (10 minutes)

Issues at the Olympics

In the past the Olympics were used to promote all that was good in sport. All competitors were amateurs, competing purely for enjoyment and although the winners received a medal it had no monetary value. However, as the modern Games moved into the second half of the twentieth century, television, especially, opened up a huge global audience. This had the effect of making the Games very attractive to commercial sponsors but also gave nations, groups and individuals a world stage on which to make their point.

Women at the Olympics

Women were not allowed to compete in the Ancient Games and when de Coubertin revived the modern Games in 1896 he too upheld this feature. Women did, however, compete at the 1900 Games, but only in two sports – tennis and golf. Gradually the number of women competing and events open to women has increased, though by 1936 there were still only four sports available to women.

By the time the Olympics were held in Sydney in 2000 there were 28 sports and 116 events for women, however, there were still twice as many male competitors as women.

Much of the early reluctance to allow women to compete at the Games was due to the philosophy of Baron de Coubertin, the founder of the modern Games. De Coubertin's opinions on women and sport were influenced by the model of the Ancient Greek Games.

There were no women at the Ancient Greek Games – either as competitors or spectators, and in the early years of the modern Olympics, the prevailing social pattern was still inclined towards keeping women very firmly in their domestic place. Fortunately, in England, Europe and the USA, women had begun to involve themselves in a range of gymnastic and sporting activities.

The opening of the track and field events to women at the Games of 1928 was highly significant. Annoyed at the refusal of the IOC to include women's athletics in the 1924 Games, a French woman, Alice Milliat, threatened to set up a rival women's organisation. This caused the IAAF to step in very quickly and endorse women's athletics. The IOC responded by including athletics for women in the 1928 Games which put women's sport at the centre of the Olympic and world stage.

In the 1970s changing attitudes towards women in society suddenly meant it became acceptable for the sporting female also to be attractive. A host of female athletes like Olga Korbut, Nadia Comaneci and Nelli Kim became household names and helped to promote female participation in sport.

Checkpoint 1

Why do you think that women were allowed to compete in tennis and golf at the 1900 Olympic Games?

Checkpoint 2

Why did the inclusion of track and field events for women at the 1928 Olympics have such a impact on female participation at the Games?

Beauty and grace are still almost unavoidably associated with many women's sporting activities. This, of course, is a societal trait rather than an Olympic one, but it does mean that sports that portray feminine qualities tend to dominate the modern Olympic Games.

Although female participation at the Games is on the up, membership of the IOC is still very much dominated by men.

Politics ●●●

The Olympic Games generates a huge media and spectator following which unfortunately means that many have used the Games to make political protests. At one extreme, states have not allowed their athletes to compete in order to make a political point against other competing nations, this is known as a boycott and the Games of 1956, 1976, 1980 and 1984 were severely affected by boycotts.

The essential element of the Olympics is that it brings together athletes and nations of the world, on the whole this is a very positive experience, reflecting de Coubertin's original ideal of building a more peaceful world through sport.

Smaller groups have used the Games to make more spontaneous statements. At the 1968 Games two black American sprinters made a 'black power' protest on the podium, knowing that the world's media were watching. Problems such as the terrorist attacks at the 1972 Olympics and later at the 1996 Atlanta Games now means that the security and safety systems at the Olympic Games have become very complex and very expensive.

Using the Olympics as a world stage for protest

© Bettmann/Corbis

Checkpoint 3

What is meant by the term 'boycott' in sport?

Checkpoint 4

Rome was the first televised Olympics in 1964, what effect did the increased TV coverage of the Games have in terms of protest?

Exam question   answer: page 50

Explain how and why groups have used the Olympic Games to stage political protests. Refer to an example in your answer.   (10 minutes)

Answers
The social contemporary study of sport

Sport, leisure and recreation: key concepts

Checkpoints

1 Four labour-saving devices that have enabled people who do housework to have more leisure time are: washing machines, dishwashers, tumble dryers, microwaves.
2 A definition of leisure, for professional sports performers, is difficult because these people work within the leisure industry and there is no demarcation between leisure and work.
3 Factors that have led to an increased participation of outdoor sports are: increase in car ownership and ease of access. TV programmes and fashion have also made it popular among young people.
4 The advantages of outdoor education over normal lessons in the inculcation of social skills are: decision making is more important in outdoor education, there is always an element of risk.

Exam question

The main differences between an activity that is a sport and one that is physical education is that sport is a competitive activity, undertaken freely by individuals and groups, it has set rules and time constraints. Physical education takes place within educational institutions and involves a teacher passing on knowledge to a group of pupils.

Sport and culture

Checkpoints

1 Colonialisation was the invasion and control of developing cultures by the British Empire during the nineteenth century.
2 The term nation building with relation to sport means using sporting success to motivate and develop pride among a country's population. Sporting success can also enhance a country's international reputation.
3 Often the armed forces act as sports nurseries by providing training and equipment for élite performers and they can also screen for sports talent.
4 Ethnic sports are traditional events that are unique to a particular geographical or cultural area.

Exam question

Sport can be used for social mobility by emergent athletes because sport can bring extrinsic rewards in terms of money and social status. Many emergent athletes will move to the West where contracts and fees are much higher.

Sport in advanced societies

Checkpoints

1 The American Dream is the idea that anyone in America can move from rags to riches, a reflection of a meritocracy – the harder you work the more you are rewarded.
2 Examples of British sport being Americanised are: teams now have nicknames and logos, cheerleaders, entertainment, increasing power of TV.
3 New World cultures tend to play sports that originated in the UK because they were all former colonies of the British Empire.
4 Australia has placed so much emphasis on developing sports talent because their sporting success counteracts their country's lack of tradition and history.

Exam question

Win ethic dominates as it reflects the Americanisation of sport, capitalist society tends to reinforce the survival of the fittest mentality, commercialism based on success, advertisers only want to be associated with successful athletes. A business attitude now dominates sport – win or bust.

Élite sport

Checkpoints

1 The term 'shop window' means that sport is used to show off a country.
2 The advantages and disadvantages of basing performers in sports schools are: *Advantages* – use best possible resources and facilities for training, have access to quality coaching, often on a one-to-one basis, work in an atmosphere of excellence, you are surrounded by talented performers. Sports science support will be available.
   Disadvantages – away from home, family and friends, chance of burn-out or over-use injuries, out of traditional club network, less emphasis on academic education.
3 The UKSI network allows international performers to use top-quality facilities for training.
4 Three key stages in the development of sporting talent are:
   1 Selection of talent.
   2 Development of talent.
   3 Providing support for performance.

Exam question

Commitment
National Lottery/World Class performance funds/National governing bodies are giving athletes grants to allow them to train full time, many schools and colleges are now developing academies so that students can combine study and élite sport preparation.

Resources
The UKSI network of institutes provides athletes with top-class training facilities and monitoring equipment, Lottery funding is also available for equipment.

Expertise
Lottery and World Class funding have appointed a number of full-time coaches and performance directors, there is also a wealth of expertise and talent at each of the UKSIs.

Ethics and values in high-level sport

Checkpoints

1 The term deviance, when used in sport, means that participants break the rules.
2 Extrinsic rewards in sport can include money, trophies, cups and medals, sponsorship deals, league points.
3 Sportsmanship is playing to the rules and spirit of the game whereas gamesmanship is where you use whatever means you can to overcome your opponent.
4 A drug in sport is any chemical substance which is taken to improve performance.

Exam question

Written rules are those published and agreed by the sports governing body. Often there will be an official referee or umpire to uphold these rules. If a player breaks these rules they will be penalised or punished. Unwritten rules, often referred to as the 'spirit of the game', require players to respect their opponents and officials, play competitively but fairly and recognise that to win by unfair advantage undermines sport. Shaking hands with your opponent at the end of the game is an example of the unwritten rules.

Sport and mass participation

Checkpoints

1 The benefits of mass participation in sport for *individuals* include improvements to fitness and health, self-confidence and a feeling of achievement.
2 The benefits of mass participation in sport for a *country* include a fitter and healthier population, integration of different cultures and races, reduction in crime, economic benefits and a feeling of national pride.
3 The concept of Sport for All first emerged from the Nordic countries and Germany.
4 The four levels of the performance pyramid are: foundation, participation, performance and excellence.

Exam question

Possible benefits for individuals and community through participation in sport would include:
Individuals – feeling fitter, improvement in health and lifestyle, less likely to suffer from illness or disease, develop sense of achievement/self-esteem/confidence.
Community – fitter population, fitter workforce, less money needed to be spent on healthcare, productivity at work should increase, reduction in crime/antisocial behaviour, feeling of pride in community.

Factors affecting participation

Checkpoints

1 Three factors that lead to discrimination in sport are:
   1 Provision – where to play
   2 Opportunity – chance to play
   3 Esteem – what will the performer feel like.
2 Provision in sport relates to a person's access to facilities and sport equipment.
3 Sports clubs can act as a barrier to participation because they work on membership systems and membership is controlled either by the ability to pay the fees or, in cases such as some golf clubs, election to the club membership. This often closes membership to certain people in the community.
4 Self-fulfilling prophecies develop from stereotypes and myths, the people they discriminate against come to believe they are valid and so conform to the stereotypes by displaying their appointed characteristics and choosing the sports that fit them.

Exam question

A person's opportunity to participate in sport can be affected by socio-cultural factors. For instance a number of personal factors can affect access to sport, these include, gender, age, social status, ethnic background and disability. Provision – where to play; opportunity – chance to play; esteem – what will the performer feel like.

The Olympic Games

Check points

1 The Olympic Oath reinforces the concept of sportsmanship, playing to the laws and spirit of sport, a key feature that de Coubertin wanted to promote at the Games.
2 De Coubertin's ideals behind the setting up of the modern Olympics were to promote international friendship through sports competition.
3 The IOC generates most of the funds it needs from commercial sponsorship from the TOP sponsors and media fees.

Exam questions

1 The Games now attract a huge global audience and this attracts commercial sponsors, the cost of the Games now runs into billions. Cities or states are unable to fund this without commercial input. In 1984 Uberroth showed that the Games could make a profit through the TOP programme and media fees.

2 The Games are still the largest gathering of people and are watched by 90 per cent of the world's population, but wars have continued throughout the modern Olympic era and many Games have been disrupted by political protest. Many states now see sporting success as a major focus for national building.

Issues at the Olympics

Checkpoints

1 Women were allowed to compete in tennis and golf at the 1900 Olympics because these sports were considered feminine and acceptable by society and the IOC.

2 The inclusion of track and field events for women at the 1928 Olympics had a big impact on female participation at the Games because as there were so many different events in track and field, the numbers of female participants was bound to increase considerably.

3 The term 'boycott' in sport is the refusal of a country to compete in an international sports event, usually for political reasons.

4 The effect of increased TV coverage of the Games in terms of protest meant that the amount of protest increased as groups recognised the huge live audience their message could now reach.

Exam question

'How' and 'why' groups have used the Olympic Games to stage political protests are:

How – groups have used the Games to make symbolic protest within the Olympic stadium, examples include the black power protest.

Year	Host city	Description of protest
1936	Berlin	Germany's leader, Hitler, used the Games to showcase his Nazi views and the power of the German nation
1968	Mexico City	Two American sprinters use the medal podium to make their 'black power' protest to show their support of the civil rights campaign in the USA, millions worldwide saw the protest live on TV
1972	Munich	Palestinian terrorist take several Israeli athletes hostage in the Olympic village to protest about Israel's occupation of Arab territory. In the eventual shootout with police, nine athletes were killed. Many felt the Games should be abandoned in honour of the dead athletes, but the IOC decided the games should carry on, in order not to be seen to give in to terrorism

Year	Host city	Description of protest
1976	Montreal	The Games were boycotted by several African countries in protest against New Zealand's presence at the Games after they had played a number of rugby matches against South Africa, who at the time were banned from international sport due to their racist policy of apartheid
1980	Moscow	The USA leads a large boycott of the Games in protest at the Soviet Union's invasion of Afghanistan
1984	Los Angeles	In retaliation for the USA-led boycott of the Moscow Olympics, the Soviet Union led an Eastern bloc 'tit for tat' boycott of the Games
1988	Seoul	Three countries boycott the Games in protest at North Korea not being allowed to host any part of the Games awarded to South Korea
1996	Atlanta	A terrorist bomb kills several people enjoying a concert outside the Olympic stadium
2000	Sydney	Cathy Freeman becomes the first indigenous person to light the Olympic flame

States and national teams have undertaken systematic protest involving boycotting the Games, examples include the 1976, 1980, 1984 and 1988 Games.

Why – the Games are a global event that attract a worldwide audience, most TV companies carry live coverage, giving protests more impact. A state pulling out of sport does not affect trade or cost them any money.

Revision checklist
The social contemporary study of sport

By the end of this chapter you should be able to:

1	Discuss the key concepts used in the sociological study of sport	Confident	Not confident. **Revise** pages 30–31
2	Give example of schemes and programmes used in schools to promote participation among schoolchildren	Confident	Not confident. **Revise** pages 31–41
3	Explain how sport reflects the culture and society in which it is played	Confident	Not confident. **Revise** pages 32–35
4	Define the ethics and values evident in high-level sport	Confident	Not confident. **Revise** pages 38–39
5	Define what is meant by the term deviance in sport	Confident	Not confident. **Revise** pages 38–39
6	Define and trace the development of the term sportsmanship	Confident	Not confident. **Revise** pages 38–39
7	Discuss how the increasing commercialism of sport is affecting the ethics of sport	Confident	Not confident. **Revise** pages 38–39
8	Discuss the issue of drugs in sport	Confident	Not confident. **Revise** pages 38–39
9	Describe the structure and role of the sports councils in the UK	Confident	Not confident. **Revise** pages 40–41
10	Discuss the concept of 'sports for all'	Confident	Not confident. **Revise** pages 40–41
11	Explain the benefits of mass participation for a country	Confident	Not confident. **Revise** pages 40–41
12	Describe the different sections of the performance pyramid	Confident	Not confident. **Revise** pages 40–41
13	Explain how talented performers are nurtured and supported in the UK	Confident	Not confident. **Revise** pages 36–37
14	Discuss the factors that affect a person's access to sport and recreation	Confident	Not confident. **Revise** pages 42–43
15	Explain the application of the terms: opportunity, provision and esteem	Confident	Not confident. **Revise** pages 42–43
16	Describe how stereotypes and sports myths can lead to discrimination	Confident	Not confident. **Revise** pages 42–43
17	Give an overview of the development of the Olympic Games	Confident	Not confident. **Revise** pages 44–45
18	Describe the structure and philosophy of the modern Olympics	Confident	Not confident. **Revise** pages 44–45
19	Explain the history of women's involvement in the Olympics and how this reflects women's role in society	Confident	Not confident. **Revise** pages 46–47
20	Discuss how states and groups have used the Games to make political protests	Confident	Not confident. **Revise** pages 44–45

Exercise physiology

The energy for physical activity is released by the breaking down of adenosine triphosphate (ATP), this energy source is only stored in small amounts within the body. Consequently the body must continually reproduce ATP so that we can continue to exercise, we need to review the three methods of ATP production in the body and be able to apply the energy continuum to sporting examples.

Exam themes

→ Understanding the types of energy used in the body

→ The energy continuum

→ ATP – its role and resynthesis

→ Compare the aerobic and anaerobic energy systems

→ Investigate the energy continuum

→ Fatigue and recovery from exercise

→ The process of fitness testing

→ The principles of training

→ The components of fitness and training

→ Developing the body's aerobic capacity

→ Strength training

→ The use of ergogenic aids in improving performance

Topic checklist

AS ○ A2 ●

	AQA	EDEXCEL	OCR	WJEC
Energy concepts	●	●	●	○
Fatigue, recovery and training	●	●	●	○
Aerobic capacity and strength training	○●	●○	●	○
Flexibility	○●	○		●

Energy concepts

The body needs a constant supply of energy in order to perform everyday tasks, but when we exercise, the rate at which our body uses energy increases. The efficiency of the energy supply is one of the major factors determining athletic performance.

The energy systems

There are three ways of synthesising ATP from ADP (adenosine diphosphate) and free phosphate to ensure a constant supply of energy. All three systems work together, the dominance of any one depending on the rate at which energy is used. When the demand for energy is high and immediate then the anaerobic processes are heavily relied on. When the demand for energy is low but sustained then the aerobic process is mainly used.

The body takes in chemical energy in the form of the food we eat, this then is converted into kinetic energy which gives us movement, or is stored as potential energy.

ATP – its role and resynthesis

Adenosine triphosphate (ATP) is the only usable form of energy in the body. It is a high-energy phosphate compound made up of one molecule of adenosine and three phosphates.

ATP = Adenosine–phosphate–phosphate–phosphate

The bonds that hold the compound together are a source of quite a lot of potential energy. When ATP is broken down the bonds between the molecules are broken and energy is released. The enzyme ATPase helps to break down ATP. It is broken down into adenosine diphosphate (ADP) and free phosphate (P), so releasing the stored energy.

In order to resynthesise ATP we need to reverse the process, this is called an **endothermic** reaction since it needs energy to work.

ADP + P + **Energy** → ATP

There are three ways in which ATP can be resynthesised in the body.

1 The phosphocreatine system (ATP/PC) or alactic system.
2 The lactic acid system or glycolysis.
3 The aerobic process.

Systems 1 and 2 are anaerobic processes: they take place without oxygen. System 3 is aerobic: it requires oxygen to work.

Checkpoint 1

What form of energy is ATP and what form of energy can it be converted into?

Take note

The breakdown of ATP:
ATP → ADP + P + **Energy**

The phospho-creatine system (ATP/PC) or alactic system	The enzyme *creatine kinase* breaks down the phosphocreatine to phosphate and creatine energy is released	Phosphocreatine → P + Creatine + **Energy**
The lactic acid system or glycolysis	This process involves the *partial* breakdown of glucose, glucose-6-phosphate is formed, the enzyme phosphofructokinase aids the process	Glucose → pyruvic acid → lactic acid + 2 ATP
The aerobic system	Stage 1 aerobic glycolysis (same as anaerobic glycolysis)	Glucose → pyruvic acid → lactic acid + 2 ATP
	Stage 2 Krebs cycle	Pyruvic acid + CoA → Acetyl CoA + oxaloacetic acid = 2 ATP + hydrogen removed
	Stage 3 electron transport chain	High energy carbon bonds break to form carbon dioxide and water as well as producing energy to resynthesise 34 molecules of ATP The total yield of the aerobic system is 38 molecules of ATP

The energy continuum ●●●

We never just produce energy from one source, we tend to use a mix of systems, the degree of utilisation depends on the duration and intensity of the exercise we are undertaking. The different demands are placed on a continuum with activities requiring 100 per cent aerobic metabolism at one end and those requiring 100 per cent anaerobic metabolism at the other end. The point where we switch from one system to another is called a threshold. Traditionally the anaerobic threshold has been linked to the onset of blood lactate (OBLA), this is the point where blood lactate begins to accumulate significantly above resting levels.

Fatigue, recovery and training

Fatigue is the exhaustion of muscle resulting from prolonged exertion, recovery is the process of returning the body to its pre-exercise state. During exercise energy stores have been used and waste products created, some of these, such as lactic acid, must be removed.

The process of recovery

Replenishment of ATP and phosphocreatine stores and removal of lactic acid will take place only when additional energy is available. Elevated rates of respiration during recovery provide the energy for these processes and this in turn results in a state of EPOC.

Myoglobin acts as a store of oxygen during strenuous exercise but during intense exercise the myoglobin stores of oxygen are depleted – it takes about 0.5 litres of oxygen and one to two minutes to replenish these stores. Energy is not required for this process, but it will happen only when a 'surplus' of oxygen is being delivered to the muscles. During recovery the elevated rate of ventilation and heart rate means that additional oxygen is available for myoglobin replenishment.

Fitness testing

A variety of tests are used to assess a performer's fitness levels, we will identify these as we revise each of the main fitness components below. Performers can undergo fitness testing before, during and after a training programme. Testing at these times can achieve four important benefits: identify specific strengths of a performer, identify any weaknesses, monitor progress and provide motivation and incentive. Prior to undertaking any fitness testing, a performer must follow safety procedures and precautions to ensure that they are physiologically and psychologically prepared. In order to assess this readiness, performers will be asked to complete a Physical Activity Readiness Questionnaire (PARQ).

Principles of training

The training programme should be devised to fit individual needs. This is called systematic, one sportsperson may have more time than another person. One person may be more motivated than another person. One person's position in a team may be different from another person's. Principles of training are simply training rules that apply to the training of all the sports they attempt, to ensure that training is safe and produces the desired physiological adaptations.

The five principles of training can be best remembered by the word SPORT.

| S | SPECIFICITY | Your training is geared 'specifically' towards your sport and/or your particular position and time in season |
| P | PROGRESSION | Gradually increase your training programme in order take the athlete onto a higher level of fitness |

The jargon

Excess post-exercise oxygen consumption (EPOC) is the extra oxygen needed to restore the body to its pre-exercise state.

Checkpoint 1

What is the purpose of recovery?

Checkpoint 2

What is the role of a PARQ?

O	OVERLOAD	Means training at a worthwhile range of intensity, also known as training in your *Target Zone*
R	REVERSIBILITY	If less training takes place, or if one stops training because of injury, the athlete loses fitness
T	TEDIUM	Make the sessions different and enjoyable. When boredom sets in it is very difficult to motivate oneself to try and improve one's fitness

Linked to the above is the FITT principle.

F	FREQUENCY	How many times per week you need to train in order to improve your fitness
I	INTENSITY	How hard you train. Train at an intensity that will take your pulse into the *Target Range*
T	TIME	How long each session must be in order to be of any benefit and to achieve improvement
T	TYPE	What sort of training you do

The components of fitness and training ●●●

There are five principle training methods:

→ **Interval training** – This involves periods of work followed by periods of rest.
→ **Continuous training** – In continuous training, the athlete does not stop working.
→ **Fartlek training** – Means '*speed play*', it is a combination of fast and slow running.
→ **Circuit training** – Involves a number of exercises set out so you avoid exercising the same muscle group consecutively.
→ **Weight training** – Uses progressive resistance, either in the form of actual weight lifted or in terms of the number of times the weight is lifted.

Included in any training schedule are:

1 The number of exercises.
2 The exercises for each muscle group.
3 The weight/intensity of the effort used.
4 The number of repetitions.
5 The number of sets.
6 How fast the exercise is done.
7 How long the rest is between sets.
8 The frequency of training.

Checkpoint 3

What is meant by the term 'target zone'?

Checkpoint 4

What is the difference between maximal and sub-maximal training and testing?

Exam questions   answers: page 62

1   What precautions and procedures should an athlete follow before undertaking any form of fitness testing?   (5 minutes)

2   Outline the methods an athlete can employ to aid their recovery after intense physical activity.   (7 minutes)

Aerobic capacity and strength training

Cardiovascular fitness is the ability to exercise the entire body for long periods of time. It requires a strong heart and clear blood vessels to supply the muscles with plenty of oxygen via the blood. Cardiovascular fitness has some benefit to all sports people as it concerns the fitness of the most important muscle in the body, the heart.

VO_2 max – the key measure

The best measure of cardiovascular fitness is called maximum oxygen uptake or VO_2 max. This measures the ability of the heart, lungs and blood to transport oxygen to the muscles. It can be measured using a number of fitness tests but the most common is the multi-stage fitness test which gives athletes a predicted VO_2 max

The multi-stage fitness test ●●●

Involves running back and forward along a 20-metre zone, the speed of running is controlled by a series of pre-recorded beeps played back through a CD or cassette player. The aim of the test is to run for as long as possible, continuing until you are unable to keep up with the beeps. The level at which you stop running gives you your cardiovascular score which can then be converted to give a predicted VO_2 max. Criticism of the test points to the fact that motivation plays an important part in how long the performer keeps running, it is also very specific to running sports. Other common tests used to measure aerobic capacity are the Harvard step test and the 12-minute Cooper Run.

Physiological adaptations of aerobic training ●●●

The aim of all training methods is to produce long-term physiological adaptations.

Sustained aerobic training should result in the following physiological adaptations:

→ Hypertrophy of the myocardium.
→ Increase in stroke volume and cardiac output.
→ Decrease in resting heart rate.
→ Increase in lung volume and maximum minute ventilation.
→ An increase in blood volume and elasticity of the vascular system.
→ Increase in muscle myoglobin and the number of mitochondria and stores of energy.

Strength ●●●

Strength is the ability of a muscle to exert force and overcome resistance. It is an essential element of many sporting skills. There are actually a number of different types of strength.

Checkpoint 1

How is maximum oxygen uptake usually presented in a shortened form?

Checkpoint 2

Describe how an increase in stroke volume and cardiac output would have a beneficial effect on aerobic capacity.

The jargon

Hypertrophy is an increase in the size of a tissue or organs.

Type of strength	Description	Sports application
Strength endurance	The ability of a muscle to work for a long period of time	Press-ups
Maximum strength	The greatest force that can be exerted in a single maximum voluntary contraction	Bench press in weight training
Explosive strength	Ability to expend energy on one explosive act	Javelin throw
Static/isometric strength	Greatest amount of force held for a period of time	Rugby scrum
Dynamic strength	Ability to exert muscular force repeatedly over time	Sprinting

Strength can be measure by a number of methods: the most common are maximal lift or using a grip dynamometer. Endurance strength can be measured using the sit-up test developed by Sports Coach UK, dynamic strength can be measured using the vertical jump test.

Physiological adaptations of strength training ●●●

Depending on the intensity and duration of the sessions, strength training can produce both aerobic and anaerobic adaptations. Aerobic adaptation would result from low weights and many repetitions could result in hypertrophy of the slow twitch muscle fibres, an increase in muscle mitochondria and myoglobin, capillarisation and a general increase in energy stores.

The jargon

Capillarisation is the development of the capillary network in a part of the body.

Checkpoint 3

What is capillarisation and what beneficial effect does it have in terms of the cardiovascular system?

Checkpoint 4

Can you think of three examples in sport that require static, explosive and dynamic strength?

Action point

Make sure you can identify the energy system that would be utilised by each type of strength.

Exam question   answer: page 62

Outline the long-term physiological adaptations in the skeleton, muscular and circulatory systems that would occur as a result of marathon training.

(10 minutes)

Flexibility

This type of fitness links both the muscular and skeletal systems. Muscles that are not stretched regularly become tight, causing pain when we stretch them. Flexibility is important in most sports, as not only does it allow a greater range of movement but it also helps prevent injury.

Types of flexibility

There are again a number of types of flexibility:

Static flexibility is the range of movement possible around a joint. **Dynamic flexibility** is the range of motion that can be achieved by actively moving a joint by force.

Flexibility can be affected by a range of factors including the joint type and the elasticity and length of the surrounding connective tissue. The most common methods of measuring flexibility are the sit-and-reach test or using a goniometer. A loss of flexibility can be caused by problems in the joints such a worn-down cartilage or a lack of synovial fluid.

There are three main methods of flexibility training:

→ **Static stretching** includes a further two methods: **active** where a joint is stretched by the áthlete actively contracting the antagonistic muscles to push the joint past its point of resistance and **passive stretching** which involves using an external force, usually gravity or a partner, to produce the stretch in the muscles.
→ **Ballistic stretching** produces a stretch using bouncing or swinging movements, this should be done with care since it can result in muscle tears and tissue damage.
→ **Proprioceptive neuromuscular facilitation (PNF)** usually performed with a partner and involving a pattern of alternating contraction and relaxation of the muscles being stretched.

Physiological adaptations of flexibility training

The aim of sustained fitness training is to develop elasticity in the tendons, ligaments and muscles surrounding the joints. The resting length of these structures will also be increased.

Other elements of fitness

There are a number of other fitness components that can contribute towards an athlete's fitness, the main ones are listed below.

Checkpoint 1

What are the benefits on improving an athlete's flexibility?

Checkpoint 2

Explain why PNF stretching is said to be more effective than other forms of stretching.

Fitness component	Description	Training methods
Balance	Ability to distribute weight of the body evenly and maintain equilibrium	Use of balance board or beam
Coordination	Putting relevant motor programmes in the right order to produce efficient smooth movement	Ball catch task Batak board
Agility	The ability to rapidly and accurately change the direction of the entire body	Illinois agility run
Reaction time	The ability to respond quickly to a stimuli	Ruler drop Batak board Computer simulators
Speed	The ability to perform a movement quickly	60m sprint Plyometrics

Ergogenic aids

An ergogenic aid is any that improves performance and with the demands of modern-day sport and the fact that the difference between winning and losing could be fractions of a second, most élite athletes are constantly looking for aids that can give their performance an edge. There is much debate in sport about the legal and ethical background to the use of ergogenic aids. Currently the use of a vast number of performance enhancing drugs is banned. However, a range of supplements and other chemical aids are allowed.

Current examples of ergogenic aids include:

→ Nutrition manipulation
  → carbo-loading
  → taking creatine supplements
→ Boosting the body's red blood cell count
  → altitude training
  → blood doping
  → use of hypoxic chambers
  → taking banned Rh EPO.

Exam questions answers: pages 62–63

1 Describe how an endurance athlete might manipulate their dietary plans during the final week before an event.   (10 minutes)

2 Explain the benefits of an athlete taking creatine as a dietary supplement when preparing for competition.   (5 minutes)

Checkpoint 3

Suggest why agility is such an important component of so many sports.

Examiner's secrets

These elements do need to be studied in depth but it would be useful if you were aware of the contribution they can make to an athlete's performance and also be able to give examples of how they can be improved.

Checkpoint 4

Outline the possible physiological benefits of altitude training in an endurance athlete.

The jargon

Erythropoietin (*EPO*) is a naturally occurring hormone that stimulates red blood cell production, a number of athletes have been caught recently taking REPO, a synthetic version in an attempt to illegally boost their oxygen-carrying capacity.

Action point

Try and keep up to date with the technical developments in sport, you will always get credit for using contemporary examples in your exam answers.

Answers
Exercise physiology

Energy concepts

Checkpoints

1 ATP energy is potential/chemical energy and it can be converted into kinetic/mechanical energy.
2 The three processes that are used to synthesise ATP are: the phosphocreatine system (ATP/PC) or alactic system; the lactic acid system or glycolysis; and the aerobic system.
3 Aerobic glycolysis takes place in the mitochondria.
4 The term 'lactate threshold' is the point at which lactic acid begins to accumulate rapidly in the blood, also called the anaerobic threshold.

Exam questions

1 Energy continuum, where activity requires a combination of the energy systems, 1500 metres at an élite level. Four minutes of exercise will use ATP/PC at the start and end of the race, the last stage will also see the athlete use the lactic acid system in the sprint to the line, if most of the race is run at a moderate pace then the aerobic system will supply the majority of the energy required.
2 The lactic acid system, anaerobic glycolysis, glucose is broken down into pyruvic acid, releasing two molecules of ATP for each molecule of glucose used. It supplies energy for high intensity for around one minute.

Fatigue, recovery and training

Checkpoints

1 Recovery is the period following physical activity in which the body's systems repair damaged tissue and replenish energy stores.
2 The role of PARQ (a pre-test questionnaire) is to ensure that performers are physiologically and psychologically prepared for testing.
3 A target zone is a specific level of intensity that an athlete needs to work at to obtain a specific physiological adaptation.
4 The difference between maximal and sub-maximal training and testing are: maximal are where subjects work to exhaustion, whereas sub-maximal is where an individual works towards a pre-set level which is below their maximum.

Exam questions

1 Athletes should undertake a PARQ and thoroughly warm up before any physical activity. The athlete needs to be physiologically and psychologically prepared for testing or training.
2 Methods to aid recovery include massage which help stimulate blood flow, a thorough cool-down to prevent blood pooling and help remove the waste products, use of ice baths or ice jackets again to stimulate blood flow, hot and cold showers to facilitate nervous and vascular activity in the muscles.

Aerobic capacity and strength training

Checkpoints

1 The maximum oxygen uptake is usually presented in shortened form: VO_2 max.
2 Increased stroke volume means that the volume of blood pumped out of the left ventricle increases and an increase in cardiac output means that there is more blood available to the body, and it is moving faster around the body.
3 Capillarisation is the development of the capillary network in a part of the body, and would include increasing the absolute number of capillaries and the capillary density, which gives a greater surface area available for the transfer of nutrients and waste products so making the vascular system more efficient.
4 Three examples on sport that require static, explosive and dynamic strength are:
Static strength – rugby scrum, rings, gymnastics.
Explosive strength – bounding, jumping for a header in football, lay-up in basketball.
Dynamic strength – 100m sprinting.

Exam question

The long-term physiological changes that result from marathon training would include: increased size and number of mitochondria, increased myoglobin, increased fuel stores and oxidative enzymes, increased efficiency of the lungs, hypertrophy of the heart, capillarisation and an increase in blood volume.

Flexibility

Checkpoints

1 The benefits of increased flexibility are that it allows an athlete a greater range of movement and they become less susceptible to injury.
2 PNF stretching is more effective since the assisting partner can help put the joint in a full-stretch position and also hold it in that position for 10 to 15 seconds, ensuring that the joint moves through its full range of motion.
3 Agility is important in many sports since it allows the athlete to change direction with maximum speed and control, allowing them to evade defenders or reach a ball.
4 The benefits of altitude training include: increasing haemoglobin content and therefore increased oxygen carrying capacity; decrease in blood plasma volume; capillarisation in the muscles; and an increase in muscle myoglobin.

Exam questions

An athlete might manipulate their diet during the final week before an event as follows:
1 Carbohydrate loading, deplete and temporarily starve the body of its normal supply of carbohydrates. Glycogen

levels will be low. Saturate the body with carbohydrates three days pre-event. When the body is again exposed to normal levels of carbohydrate it will store extra glycogen, helping to extend the duration of activity for endurance events.

2 Increases PC stores in the body and therefore raises the threshold of the alactic system. Specifically aids sport where work is intermittent. The additional creatine improves recovery time. It also allows athletes to train at higher intensity for longer periods of time.

Revision checklist
Exercise physiology

By the end of this chapter you should be able to:

1	Discuss the three ways of synthesising ATP within the body and its application to sport	Confident	Not confident. **Revise** pages 54–55
2	Explain the term energy continuum and be able to give practical examples of its application in sport	Confident	Not confident. **Revise** pages 54–55
3	Describe how the knowledge of threshold can aid sports training and performance	Confident	Not confident. **Revise** pages 54–55
4	Discuss the process of recovery from exercise	Confident	Not confident. **Revise** pages 56–57
5	Discuss the concept of aerobic capacity and be able to give training methods linked to the concept	Confident	Not confident. **Revise** pages 58–59
6	Discuss the components of fitness and training	Confident	Not confident. **Revise** pages 58–61
7	Explain the principles of training	Confident	Not confident. **Revise** pages 56–57
8	Outline the physiological adaptations of aerobic training	Confident	Not confident. **Revise** pages 58–59
9	Outline the physiological adaptations of strength training	Confident	Not confident. **Revise** pages 58–59
10	Explain the importance of flexibility in most sports	Confident	Not confident. **Revise** pages 60–61
11	Discuss and give training methods for the various fitness components	Confident	Not confident. **Revise** pages 60–61
12	Give examples of ergogenic aids in sport	Confident	Not confident. **Revise** pages 60–61

The biomechanical analysis of human movement

All motion in sporting activity, whether it's the movement of the performer's body or some object of equipment such as a projectile, behaves in accordance with a well-established set of scientific principles and mechanical laws. In this chapter we will revise the application of these principles and laws to sporting movement. If possible you need to apply all these principles to sporting activities, preferably sports that you yourself have performed or studied. Although the least popular choice in advanced PE exams, this should be a straightforward unit to revise. Do not forget to take a calculator into your exam and brush up on your maths skills as most biomechanics questions usually include some calculation.

Exam themes

→ Definitions and laws of motion

→ Measuring and presenting linear motion

→ The concept of momentum

→ The types of forces acting on sports performers

→ Air resistance and fluid friction

→ Flight and characteristics of projectiles

→ The mechanics of stability

→ The concept of angular motion in sport

Topic checklist

AS ○ A2 ●

	AQA	EDEXCEL	OCR	WJEC
Definitions and laws of motion	○ ●	●	●	○
Momentum	●	●	●	○
The mechanics of stability and motion	●	●	●	○

Definitions and laws of motion

Every body continues in its state of rest, or of uniform motion in a straight line, except in so far as it may be compelled by impressed forces to change that state.

Newton's First Law of Motion

Checkpoint 1

How do we calculate acceleration?

Example

The most common sporting example of Newton's third law is a sprinter's start blocks, when the sprinter pushes out of the blocks there is a resultant opposite and equal force pushing the sprinter forward off the blocks.

Checkpoint 2

What are the correct units of measurement for speed, velocity and acceleration?

Take note

Pure linear motion is rarely seen in most sports events but it can often be apparent in sporting actions such as sprinting.

The jargon

Velocity is the rate at which a body moves, it is a vector quantity in that it possesses both magnitude and direction.

The jargon

Scalar quantity is a physical quantity that is described completely in terms of its magnitude.

The jargon

Displacement is the distance an object has moved in a given direction.

In sport motion is produced only when force is applied, the main sources of this force are:

→ **Internal** – the muscular system of the athlete contracting to produce force
→ **External** – this could include gravity, friction of fluid or surface or resistance of the air.

Types of motion in sport

Motion is of two kinds:
Linear motion is the progression of a body in a straight line with all its parts moving in the same distance, same direction and at the same speed. **Angular motion** is the more common type, where a body rotates about a fixed point. Often in sport the most efficient movement requires a combination of linear and angular motion.

Newton's laws of motion are fundamental to an understanding of how these elements combine to effect sporting performance.

Newton's First Law of Motion, the law of inertia, states that an object will remain at rest unless acted on by an external source, also if the object is moving then it will do so in the same direction and at the same velocity unless acted upon by an external force.

Newton's Second Law of Motion, the law of acceleration, states that when a body is acted on by a force, its resulting change in momentum takes place in the direction in which the force is applied and is in proportion to the force causing it and inversely proportional to its mass. This is often expressed by the following formulae $a = f/m$.

Newton's Third Law of Motion, the law of reaction, states that for every action there is an equal and opposite reaction, therefore when one object exerts a force on another, there will be an equal force exerted in the opposite direction by the second object on the first.

Measuring and presenting linear motion

The three main components linked to linear motion are:

→ **Speed** is distance travelled per unit time measured in ms^{-1}, speed is a scalar quantity and is calculated thus speed = distance/time
→ **Velocity** is the rate at which a body moves, it is a vector quantity in that it possesses both magnitude and direction. It is measured in ms^{-1} and is calculated thus: velocity = displacement/time
→ **Acceleration** is the rate of change in velocity and is therefore a vector quantity, it is measured in ms^{-2} and is calculated thus: acceleration = change in velocity/time taken to change.

Often linear motion qualities in sport are presented as graphic descriptions:

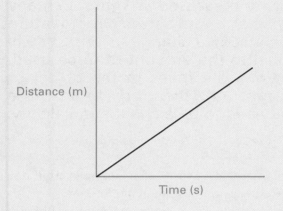

This graph represents steady speed

Checkpoint 3

What does a horizontal line on a distance v time graph represent?

This graph with a horizontal line represents stationary

Checkpoint 4

Explain the difference between scalar and vector qualities.

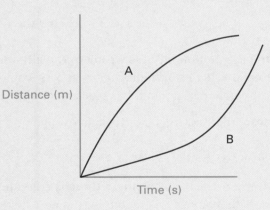

On this graph line A represents deceleration and line B represents acceleration

Action point

Make sure you know the correct units for speed, velocity and acceleration.

Exam question   answer: page 72

1   In sport people and objects rarely travel at constant speed. Sketch and
    label four separate distance v time graphs showing the following:
    (i)   steady speed
    (ii)   stationary
    (iii) acceleration
    (iv)   deceleration.

                                                            (10 minutes)

Momentum

Momentum is the product of mass and velocity ($M = mv$), it is a vector quantity and can be considered as a measure of the quantity of motion possessed by a body. Momentum is measured as kgm^{-1}. In many sports athletes attempt to optimise their momentum but as the second law states, a change in velocity will be directly proportional to the amount of force used. In most sports situations the mass of the object or performer remains constant, therefore to increase momentum there will need to be a change in velocity.

Force

Force is defined as the pushing or pulling effect of an action exerted on an object often resulting in a change in the state of motion.

Force can have a number of effects on the body: making something move, stopping something that is already moving or attempting to stop something from moving altogether. Within sport the force can be internal (created by the muscles) or external (factors such as gravity). Force is calculated using $F = ma$ and is measured in Newtons (N). When two forces act at 90° to each other the Pythagoras theory is used to calculate the resultant force, if a number of forces are acting on an object the overall effect is referred to as the reluctant force.

The effect that a force has on a body is influenced by a number of factors: the size of the force, the direction of the force and the position of application.

Force and performance

Weight calculated as $W = mg$ and measured as m/s^2, g represents the acceleration of free fall.

Friction is a force that opposes motion but it is wrong to think that it always has a negative effect on sports performance, many sports would not exist without it. In sport it can occur in a number of situations:

→ Between two solid surfaces either in terms of grip as in cycling or sliding as in skating.
→ Between an object and the air or fluid.

In all cases friction will slow an object down unless there is a greater force to counteract the friction. In many sports technology is now being harnessed to reduce the effects of friction. Examples include developing a more streamlined shape in movement and using different footwear on different surfaces.

Checkpoint 1

How can a performer increase velocity in order to increase momentum?

Checkpoint 2

What does Pythagoras' theory state?

Checkpoint 3

What is the gravitational force for most places on the globe?

Take note

Be careful not to confuse weight and mass, mass is simply the quantity of matter composing an object.

Air resistance and fluid friction ●●●

Air resistance is the frictional force which reduces the speed of a body through the air and therefore affects skills such as running and jumping. It also can cause projectiles such as a javelin or a shuttlecock to fall to the ground before they have completed their parabolic flight path. The lighter the body then the greater the resistance, the speed of the object also has an influence in that greater resistance occurs at higher speeds. Air resistance is also affected by the cross-sectional area of the object. Possible techniques that can be used to overcome the effects of air resistance in sport include streamlining through either body shape or clothing, such as the swift suit worn by sprinters, and in sports such as cycling a technique called drafting is used where performers reduce drag by following closely behind another participant.

Fluid friction is usually related to aquatic events, it is defined as the resistance of a body in a fluid due to forces of friction being exerted between the body and the fluid. Again it is mainly affected by the cross-sectional area of the object or swimmer. Swimmers work on streamlining body shapes and further reduce resistance by shaving body hair and using tight-fitting suits.

Two linked forces associated with air and fluid resistance are drag and lift. Drag occurs when air is not allowed to pass smoothly around an object. Lift occurs when there is a pressure difference in the air passing above and below an object. In sports such as cricket and tennis lift is used to create the Bernoulli and Magnus effects.

The Bernoulli Effect acts on balls and projectiles, when a pressure differential exists between upper and lower surfaces on an object a lift force will move in the direction of the area of higher pressure.

The jargon

Streamlining is making the overall shape of a body flow through a fluid or air so as to offer the smallest cross-sectional area and therefore minimise the resistance.

Checkpoint 4

What is the relationship between friction and speed?

Example

The Bernoulli Effect is what keeps the javelin in the air when it is released. The Magnus Effect is where the Bernoulli Effect is applied to spinning objects. The spin creates a region of low velocity and high pressure on one side and a region of high velocity and low pressure on the opposite side. This pressure difference creates a deviation in the direction of the projectile towards the direction of the spin.

Action point

Both the Bernoulli Effect and Magnus Effect are popular exam topics, make sure you understand the difference between the two. It is often a good idea to sketch diagrams in your answers to explain the effects, so practise this during your revision.

Checkpoint 5

Give examples of methods that sports performers can use to reduce air resistance and fluid friction.

Exam question   answer: page 72

1   Explain the concept of fluid friction and suggest three ways in which a sports performer can reduce its effects.   (7 minutes)

The mechanics of stability and motion

Checkpoint 1

Can you suggest why and how high-jumpers change their body shape to alter the centre of gravity to their advantage?

The jargon

Gravity line – this is a vertical line passing from the CoG of an object down to the ground.

Checkpoint 2

Why does a sprinter want to be in an off-balance position at the start of a race?

Checkpoint 3

Can you identify the lateral and longitudinal axes of the human body?

The jargon

Moment of inertia = mass × rotational radius^2 and is measured as kgm^2 Moment of inertia is governed by the distance of the moving body parts from the axis of rotation. The law of conservation of angular momentum, which is related to Newton's first law, states that a rotating body will continue to turn about its axis of rotation with constant angular momentum unless another force is exerted upon it.

The centre of gravity (CoG) represents the point at which weight is acting upon an object. As the human body has an irregular shape the centre of gravity cannot be easily defined and also it changes its position as the body moves and may even fall outside the body. Another term, 'centre of mass', can also be used, this refers to the point around which mass is balanced in all directions.

Stability in sport

In sport we are mainly concerned with the concept of equilibrium and stability, the stability is said to depend on whether the performer is in a state of stable equilibrium. In order to be stable a performer's CoG must be within the perimeter of the base of support. The greater the distance the CoG is from the base of support the less stable the performer will be.

Some athletes actually use an off-balance position to aid their performance, this is where they create a body shape where the CoG is on the edge of the support base, sprinters, for example, use this technique at the start of their race.

Angular motion in sport

This aspect of mechanics is focussed on rotation in sport, its study contains similar elements to the study of linear motion. For example, angular velocity is the rate of spin of an object and can be calculated as angular velocity = angle turned/time taken to turn. The actual amount of angular motion is referred to as angular momentum and is the moment of inertia × angular velocity. The moment of inertia is the force required to start or stop an object rotating.

Flight and characteristics of projectiles ●●●

The flight path of a projectile is called the trajectory and there are a number of factors which can affect the flight path of projectiles in sport before release and during the actual flight.

Before release: The speed of release, angle of release and height of release will all have an effect on the trajectory. Generally in sport the optimum angle for the projection is 45°, when its vertical and horizontal velocities will be equal. This, however, assumes that the point of release and landing are equal and obviously in sports such as athletics this is not the case, the release point is usually two metres above the landing point so there will be adjustments around this 45° figure.

During flight: In the throwing events of shot and hammer, distance is dependent upon the speed and angle of release and these will tend to follow a parabolic flight path.

In the throwing events of javelin and discus, speed, angle of release and aerodynamics determine the distance; these objects will not follow parabolic flights.

A parabolic curve

Checkpoint 4

How can the moment of inertia be increased and decreased?

The jargon

Axis of rotation – there are three axes of rotation running through the body: longitudinal, lateral and dorso-ventral.

Examiner's secrets

Try and think which sports best fit the principles and theories stated – these are likely not to be the sports used in exam questions.

Exam question answer: page 73

1 Many sports involve athletes performing rotational movement, explain in which ways the performer can control the rate at which they rotate.

(7 minutes)

Answers
The biomechanical analysis of human movement

Definitions and laws of motion

Checkpoints

1 Acceleration is calculated as the change in velocity divided by the time taken to change, $a = \frac{v-u}{t}$.
2 The correct units of measurement for speed, velocity and acceleration are: speed – ms^{-1}, velocity – ms^{-1} and acceleration – ms^{-2}.
3 A horizontal line on a distance v time graph represents stationary.
4 The difference between scalar and vector qualities are: a vector quality possesses both magnitude and direction. A scalar quality is described completely in terms of its magnitude.

Exam question

steady speed

stationary

acceleration

deceleration

Momentum

Checkpoints

1 A performer can increase velocity in order to increase momentum by increasing their speed and rate of movement, this could be done through increasing stride length and stride rate.
2 Pythagoras' theory states that for any right-angled triangle the square of the hypoteneuse is equal to the sum of the squares of the opposite two sides.
3 For most places on the globe gravitational field strength is 9.806 ms^{-2} (though is slightly reduced the nearer the equator we go).
4 The relationship between friction and speed is that as speed increases so too does friction.
5 Methods used by sports performers to reduce air resistance and fluid friction are: working on streamlining body shapes and further reducing resistance by shaving body hair and using tight-fitting suits.

Exam question

Fluid friction is a force which acts against moving objects and tends to slow down motion. Strategies to overcome it include streamlined body shapes or positions, specialist clothing and material, shaving body hair and the use of specialist equipment such as streamlined cycle helmets.

The mechanics of stability and motion

Checkpoints

1 Arching the body and raising arms in the high jump are good examples of how athletes attempt to allow CoG to pass over the bar.
2 Sprinters want to be in an off-balance position at the start of a race to maximise forward motion which will cause the athlete to fall forward from the blocks.
3 The lateral and longitudinal axes at the human body are as shown in the diagram below.

Longitudinal axis

Lateral axis

4 The moment of inertia can be altered through changing the body shape. Generally, the longer the body shape the greater the moment of inertia.

Exam question

A performer can control the rate of rotation by changing body shape; bringing body parts closer to the axis of rotation can speed up rotation – this could include piking, tucking, bringing in arms. Rotation can be slowed by moving body parts away from the axis of rotation by opening out/extending arms and legs.

Revision checklist
The biomechanical analysis of human movement

By the end of this chapter you should be able to:

1	Discuss the definitions and laws of motion	Confident	Not confident. **Revise** pages 66–67
2	Outline the different types of motion that occur in sport	Confident	Not confident. **Revise** pages 66–71
3	Explain the difference between scalar and vector quantities	Confident	Not confident. **Revise** pages 66–67
4	Calculate and define the term 'momentum in sport'	Confident	Not confident. **Revise** pages 67–69
5	Explain the forces acting on the sports performer	Confident	Not confident. **Revise** pages 70–71
6	Discuss the concept of stability in sport	Confident	Not confident. **Revise** pages 68–71
7	Be able to calculate the moment of inertia for an object	Confident	Not confident. **Revise** pages 68–69
8	Explain the Bernoulli Effect and the Magnus Effect	Confident	Not confident. **Revise** pages 68–69
9	Describe the effects of air resistance and fluid friction on objects in sport	Confident	Not confident. **Revise** pages 68–69
10	Describe the types of flight and the characteristics of projectiles	Confident	Not confident. **Revise** pages 70–71
11	Describe how the moment of inertia can be altered through changing the body shape	Confident	Not confident. **Revise** pages 70–71

Sports psychology

A successful athlete requires not just a high level of skill and the appropriate physiological conditioning, but also the right mental attitude. Those athletes who are highly skilled and at the top of their fitness for their sport may not perform at their optimal levels if they do not feel confident, are unmotivated or are stressed by the competition. The role of sport psychology is to help performers control their stress levels and emotions, mentally preparing for performance and focussing in on the most important cues for their sport. The main areas of potential limits on performance are motivation, arousal and stress management.

Exam themes

→ Personality and attitudes
→ Sports psychology and its effect on group performance
→ Group dynamics
→ Mental preparation for sport
→ Leadership in sport
→ Effects and consequences of competition
→ Emotional control
→ Social facilitation and the presence of others
→ Aggression
→ Attribution theory

Topic checklist

AS ○ A2 ●

	AQA	EDEXCEL	OCR	WJEC
Sports psychology and its effects on the individual performer	●	●	●	●
Sports psychology and its effects on group performance	●	●	●	●
Mental preparation for sport	●	●	●	●
Effects and consequences of competition	●	●	●	●

Sports psychology and its effects on the individual

Every sports performer is an individual, this makes it very difficult to predict how they will react in certain situations. However, there are a number of underlying traits that are common to us all and certain environmental influences that appear to affect us in similar ways. In this section we will review the work done on linking individual differences to sports performance.

Personality ●●●

There are many different personality types and theories.

Eysenck was one the first psychologists to investigate personality and identified two basic types, introverts and extroverts, that can be applied to sports performers.

Extroverts	Introverts
Prefer team sports	Prefer individual sports
Aggressive	Less active
Very competitive	Less competitive

Checkpoint 1

Explain the difference between the trait and social learning approaches to the study of personality.

Examiner's secrets

You need to be able to discuss the limitations of personality profiling in sport.

Trait theories of personality suggest that someone's personality is an enduring trait that influences behaviour in all situations. Whereas the narrow band approach splits personalities into two types: Type A personalities are impatient, intolerant and experience high levels of stress, whereas Type B personalities are relaxed, tolerant and have lower stress levels. Another approach called social learning suggests that a person's personality changes with the situation and that the environment around the performer influences behaviour. Interactionists believe that both the trait and social learning theories are valid – we are born with certain personality traits but these can change in given situations.

Attitudes ●●●

Attitudes are learnt predispositions that make us act in a particular way in a given situation. The triadic model identified three type of influence that form attitudes:

→ **Beliefs** – the cognitive element
→ **Emotions** – the affective element
→ **Behaviour** – the behavioural element.

Attitudes in sport and physical education can be changed through persuasion and through Festinger's theory of cognitive dissonance. This theory suggests that people like to be consistent in their thoughts and attitudes. If two cognitive elements conflict and people are motivated to reduce dissonance, they will feel more comfortable with the positive element and this will become the dominant attitude.

performer

Attitudes are mainly based around past experience and social learning, especially through vicarious experience, and we tend to follow social norms.

Often stereotypes and sporting myths can shape our behaviour.

Motivation

Motivation is often referred to in two ways:

Intrinsic motivation is the drive to do well which comes from inside yourself, often associated with enjoyment and pride.

Extrinsic motivation is a drive to do well that comes from outside, from, for instance, other people or a form of reward such as a money, prize or trophy.

Atkinson and McClelland developed the theory of achievement motivation; they identified two types of performer. Some have a greater need to achieve (*Nach*) than others and have what is known as 'approach behaviours'. People at the other end of the scale seem to avoid competitive situations because they need to avoid failure (*Naf*) and have what is known as 'avoidance' behaviours.

Nach athletes tend to	Naf athletes tend to
Have a persistent attitude – stick to the job in hand	Give up easily
Are willing to take risks	Avoid challenging situations
Take responsibility for their actions	Avoid personal responsibility
Welcome feedback about their performance	Do not want feedback about their performance

Checkpoint 2

Describe the triadic model.

The jargon

Vicarious experience is experience gained by watching other people perform.

Checkpoint 3

Explain how cognitive dissonance can change attitude.

Checkpoint 4

Would you expect Nach or Naf athletes to avoid competitive situations?

Examiner's secrets

Candidates will be expected to be able to give specific sports examples of achievement motivation.

Exam questions   answers: page 84

1   Attitude in sport affects the behaviour of both participants and spectators. Describe what is meant by the term attitude and identify influences which might shape the attitude of sports performers and spectators.   (8 minutes)

Sports psychology and its effects on group

Most sports involve groups of people performing together or supporting one another. The way that these people interact and communicate has been the focus of much psychological study. Individuals on teams and in competition will bring their own personalities but they will also be influenced by a range of others including their co-performers on the pitch as well as officials, members of the crowd, family friends and the media.

Group dynamics

Key phrases used when discussing group and teams are:

Phrase	Explanation
Group dynamics	Processes within the group and between groups
Cohesion	Forces which motivate members to stay and work for the group
Mutual awareness	Understanding the needs and aims of team members
Interaction	Interplay between members of the group
Common goal	Sharing an aim or predetermined result

Steiner developed a model which looks at the processes that operate within a team.

Actual productivity = Potential productivity – losses due to faulty processes.

Steiner also identified that two main reasons for unproductive groups are coordination problems, such as the Ringleman Effect, and motivational problems, such as social loafing. The Ringleman Effect suggests that individual performance decreases as the group size increases.

Leadership

Leaders play an important role in influencing groups and individuals as well as setting goals. In terms of sport, leaders include team captains, coaches, managers and teachers. Again there is some debate as to whether leadership is a natural trait or influenced by social learning. Carron suggested that leaders can emerge in two ways:

→ **Emergent** – from within a group because they are identified as skilful or responsible
→ **Prescribed** – appointed from an external source.

Examiner's secrets

Try and use these phrases when answering questions on group dynamics.

Checkpoint 1

What is meant by social loafing?

The jargon

Social loafing – where an individual loses motivation within a group linked to a loss of identity.

Examiner's secrets

Make sure you can offer suggestions about successful teams.

Checkpoint 2

What factors affect group cohesion?

performance

Many different types of leadership styles have been identified:

Style	Description
Task-orientated	Concerned with task the group has been given
Person-orientated	Concerned with interpersonal behaviour of the group
Authoritarian	Task-orientated and leader-centred, little or no intervention from the rest of the group
Democratic	Considered leader who encourages intervention from all team members
Laissez-faire	Takes very few decisions; lets team members do as they wish

There are preferred styles by different sports individuals and groups, though again this depends on the situation. Chelladurai identified five categories of preferred leadership styles that can be applied to performers of different ability and experience. These are training and instruction, democratic, autocratic, social support, and rewarding.

Again the actual style of leadership may alter with the situation the group is in, Fiedler's contingency model of leadership applied the dual classification of task- and person-orientated styles to a range of situations. His conclusion was that task-orientated leaders are more effective in situations that are at the extremes of favourable or unfavourable, whereas person-orientated leaders are most effective in situations that are moderately favourable.

Take note

Most leaders are actually a mix of all styles, but may tend towards one.

Checkpoint 3

What factors would make a situation more favourable for a leader?

Checkpoint 4

Describe how a group leader may emerge.

Exam questions   answers: page 84

1   Identify three leadership qualities that are important in a sports coach.
                                                            (5 minutes)

2   Autocratic and democratic styles are often used by people in a leadership position. Explain each style of leadership and suggest situations which each type may favour.   (8 minutes)

Mental preparation for sport

Stress has always been an integral part of sport, though many would argue that the amount of stress in sport in recent years has increased greatly due to the amount of sponsorship and other extrinsic rewards now available to successful performers. To begin reducing the effects of stress, sports performers need to first of all identify the source of stress and then use methods of mental preparation to help them prepare for competition.

Commitment ●●●

Goal setting can help improve a performer or team's motivation and confidence, reduce anxiety and ultimately enhance performance. There are three different types of goals:

→ **outcome goals**
→ **performance goals**
→ **process-orientated goals.**

Many élite performers and teams will set themselves long-term goals, for example, over a season, but these will be preceded by short-term goals which help control anxiety. To make goal setting more effective many now use the guide known as the SMARTER principle.

S	Specific	Goals must be clear and understood
M	Measurable	Performers must be able to check or assess how well they are progressing
A	Agreed	Goals shared with coach and team are more likely to be achieved
R	Realistic	Goals to be within the reach of the performer
T	Time-phased	Short-term goals give a step-by-step move towards long-term goals
E	Exciting	Goals must stimulate and offer rewards
R	Recorded	Goals must be written down and any progress recorded, to help with motivation

Self-confidence ●●●

Motivation is often affected by the level of self-confidence a performer has. Bandura proposed a theory of self-efficacy which suggested that self-confidence can be specific to a particular situation. There are a range of factors that affect self-efficacy: performance accomplishments, vicarious experiences, verbal persuasion and emotional arousal.

Concentration ●●●

Being able to concentrate on important cues is an essential trait for sports performers. Cue utilisation theory suggests that as an athlete's arousal increases, their attention narrows, initially filtering out irrelevant environmental cues leading to improved performance.

Checkpoint 1

Give three examples of typical stressors in sport.

The jargon

Performance accomplishments – if success has been accomplished in the past then self-confidence will be high.

Checkpoint 2

Can you think of a sports-specific example of self-efficacy?

However, if arousal continues to rise then relevant cues are also ignored, leading to a loss in performance. Psychologists identify a range of additional styles which relate to a two-dimensional model of the direction (external to internal) and width (broad to narrow) of attention.

Emotional control ●●●

Sports performance is closely linked to an athlete's level of arousal and activation. There are two main theories about the relationship between arousal level and performance. The drive theory developed by Hull suggests that there is a linear relationship, in that performance increases in proportion to arousal, thus:

The inverted U theory, developed by Yerkes and Dodson, suggests that optimum performance is reached at moderate arousal levels, but at low and high arousal levels performance decreases. Each individual performer will have a unique level of optimum arousal and this may change according to the situation.

Often athletes become anxious before competitive events, this is referred to as stress and it can have both positive and negative effects on performance. Anxiety is a negative form of stress. There are two types of anxiety: **trait anxiety** – an enduring tendency to exhibit anxiety and **state anxiety**, the anxiety actually experienced in a particular situation. In sport we are mainly concerned with anxiety associated with competition; Marten developed the SCAT test which can be used to measure competitive anxiety.

Managing stress is therefore an important skill for athletes to master. At the outset, identifying signs of stress are useful; two types of state anxiety have been recognised: **somatic anxiety** (stress response of the body) and **cognitive anxiety** (stress response of the mind). There are a number of techniques that are useful for controlling both types of anxiety.

Imagery	Visualising success or enjoyment
Self-talk	Using key word and phrases to maintain focus and concentration
Relaxation	Tensing muscles to relax parts of the body

Exam questions   answers: page 84

1   Anxiety is the negative aspect of stress. Explain what is meant by the terms somatic and cognitive anxiety.   (5 minutes)

2   Name and describe one cognitive technique of stress management.
(4 minutes)

The jargon

Cue – a signal for some particular action, may be verbal, visual or kinaesthetic.

Checkpoint 3

How should a coach utilise knowledge of the inverted U theory of arousal when motivating a sports team for an important match?

The jargon

Activation – the state of readiness of an individual to respond to a stimulus or cue.

Checkpoint 4

Describe what is meant by 'state and trait anxiety'.

Examiner's secrets

Many questions will ask for strategies that can be used to reduce anxiety – make sure you have lots of examples.

Effects and consequences of competition

Competition is the main focus for most people in sport and this brings in another range of factors that affect confidence and motivation. The presence of others raises arousal levels which can have either a positive or negative effect on performance. Again in order to be successful, performers need to identify the effects that competition can have on their own performance and then develop coping strategies to cope with any negative effects.

Social facilitation and audience effect

Social facilitation is the influence other people can have on an individual's performance. These 'others' could include other performers/co-actors or an audience, either live or via TV. Zajonc suggests that the presence of others raises arousal levels, which can have a positive or negative effect on performance, and this can be linked to drive theory, with the dominant response being more likely in high arousal situations. This would create a positive response for experts, extroverts or during simple or gross skills. But would produce a negative response in beginners, introverts and during fine and complex skills. The presence of others can also cause evaluation apprehension where others are evaluating performance.

Aggression

Aggression is a term that is loosely used in sport. Again it can have both a positive and negative effect on performance, Aggression is literally 'intent to harm outside the laws of the game'. Where aggression is controlled or channelled it becomes assertion and it is this concept we should encourage in sport. There are a number of theories that suggest causes for aggression and again they tend to fall into the two camps of **nature** or **nurture**. The instinct theory suggests that aggression is an innate biological drive and sport simply gives an outlet for this aggression. The frustration–aggression hypothesis is a version of the drive theory which states that blocking goals can cause frustration which then leads to aggression. The social learning theory developed by Bandura states that we learn to be aggressive by watching others. Strategies to reduce aggression include internal control of arousal levels, punishment and the reinforcement of non-aggressive behaviour.

Consequences of sports performance ●●●

Attribution theory

Attributions are the reasons we give for winning or losing, they can be linked to motivation and therefore have an important effect on future performance. Weiner developed a model which gives four main reasons for a result, thus:

	Locus of causality	
	Internal cause	External cause
Stable cause	Ability	Task difficulty
Unstable cause	Effort	Luck

Often beginners or performers who do not gain consistent success can develop learned helplessness. Often failure is attributed to uncontrollable factors. Attribution retraining can help to change attributions and minimise the effects of learned helplessness.

Checkpoint 3

What can create learned helplessness in a performer?

Checkpoint 4

In what ways can learned helplessness be changed into a positive attribute?

Exam question   answer: page 85

For most athletes the presence of an audience leads to a rise in arousal levels. Outline the positive and negative effects that an audience may have on performance and state how this may differ depending on the level of the performer.   (10 minutes)

Answers
Sports psychology

Sports psychology and its effects on the individual performer

Checkpoints

1 Trait theories of personality suggest that someone's personality is an enduring trait that influences behaviour in all situations, whereas social learning suggests that a person's personality changes with the situation and that the environment around the performer influences behaviour.

2 The triadic model identified three types of influence that form attitudes:
Beliefs – the cognitive element
Emotions – the affective element
Behaviour – the behavioural element.

3 Cognitive dissonance can change attitude. By making all three elements stable, and changing attitude, an individual must experience two or more opposing beliefs and make one of these beliefs dominant.

4 Naf athletes would tend to avoid competitive situations.

Exam question

1 An attitude in sport is a predisposition towards an attitude subject. Influences include previous participant and spectator experiences, vicarious experiences, influence from the media presence of TV and/or crowd reactions, cultural and religious factors, the behaviour of peers and significant others.

Sports psychology and its effects on group performance

Checkpoints

1 Social loafing is the reduction in individual effort and motivation as the group size increases.

2 Factors that affect group cohesion include having shared goals, success of performance, level of social friendship and the effectiveness of the leadership.

3 Factors that would make a situation more favourable for a leader are good relationships between leader and group, a clear and easy to understand task, a leader who has authority and respect.

4 A group leader may emerge by prescription, or be elected by external factors or emerge from within the group through peer support.

Exam questions

1 Leadership qualities that are important in a sports coach are: they must be well motivated, have a vision or set goal, are a good communicator, show empathy and respect for the group members, are a skilful performer, have a good knowledge of their sport, have a natural talent for leadership.

2 An autocratic style is task-orientated and didactic. It is best in dangerous situations and with larger groups. A democratic style is person-orientated where the emphasis is on human relations and on encouraging others to participate in decision making. Works best in small groups or with individuals and with highly skilled groups.

Mental preparation for sport

Checkpoints

1 Three examples of typical stressors include competition, conflict and frustrations.

2 An example of self-efficacy in sport is athletes showing a large degree of self-confidence.

3 A coach can utilise their knowledge of the inverted U theory of arousal by recognising that every individual member of the team has a different optimum level of performance and may need different means of reaching this level.

4 Trait anxiety is an enduring tendency to exhibit anxiety and state anxiety is the anxiety actually experienced in a particular situation.

Exam questions

1 Somatatic anxiety is the physiological effect of stress, manifest in a rise in heart rate and higher adrenaline levels. Cognitive anxiety is the psychological effect manifest as high irritability and a feeling of apprehension.

2 Cognitive techniques of stress management are: imagery, positive thinking, selective attention or mental rehearsal.

Effects and consequences of competition

Checkpoints

1 Social facilitation is the influence other people can have on an individual's performance.

2 The instinct theory suggests that aggression is an innate biological drive and sport simply gives an outlet for this aggression. The frustration–aggression hypothesis is a version of the drive theory which states that blocking goals can cause frustration which then leads to aggression. The social learning theory developed by Bandura states that we learn to be aggressive by watching others.

3 Past experiences/failures which lead performer to believe that failure is inevitable and belief that failure is due to uncontrollable factors can create learned helplessness in a performer.
4 Learned helplessness can be changed into a positive attribute by retraining to give success, reinforcing good performance, offering positive feedback – these all help to attribute success to stable controllable factors.

Exam question

The positive or negative effects that an audience may have on performance are: a positive effect may occur on gross/simple/group/low in organisation activity and the more highly skilled or experienced the athlete the more positive the effect. A negative effect on fine/complex/individual activities that require concentration and focus may occur, and this will be magnified if the performer is a beginner, inexperienced or novice.

Revision checklist
Sports psychology

By the end of this chapter you should be able to:

1	Discuss the different personality types and theories	Confident	Not confident. **Revise** pages 76–77
2	Discuss the difference between introvert and extrovert personalities	Confident	Not confident. **Revise** pages 76–77
3	Explain what factors can affect group cohesion in sport	Confident	Not confident. **Revise** pages 78–79
4	Explain the differences between intrinsic and extrinsic motivation	Confident	Not confident. **Revise** pages 76–77
5	Explain the differences between Nach and Naf athletes	Confident	Not confident. **Revise** pages 76–77
6	Understand the application of the theories of group dynamics in sport	Confident	Not confident. **Revise** pages 78–79
7	Describe what is meant by the term social loafing	Confident	Not confident. **Revise** pages 78–79
8	Explain the different types of leadership styles	Confident	Not confident. **Revise** pages 78–79
9	Describe how motivation can be affected by the level of self-confidence	Confident	Not confident. **Revise** pages 80–81
10	Outline the theory of goal setting and the use of the SMARTER principles	Confident	Not confident. **Revise** pages 80–81
11	Explain the inverted U theory and its application to sport	Confident	Not confident. **Revise** pages 80–81
12	Describe how athletes can measure and manage stress	Confident	Not confident. **Revise** pages 80–81
13	Discuss the concept of social facilitation and audience effect on sports performance	Confident	Not confident. **Revise** pages 82–83
14	Explain the theories and application of the concept of aggression in sport	Confident	Not confident. **Revise** pages 82–83
15	Discuss the practical application of attribution theory to sport	Confident	Not confident. **Revise** pages 82–83
16	Explain what can create learned helplessness and suggest ways learned helplessness can be changed into a positive attribute	Confident	Not confident. **Revise** pages 82–83

Historical study of physical education and sport

This chapter includes the study of the historical development of sport, reviews the development on society and its effect on sport over the last 500 years. The initial phase of the development of sport was in pre-industrial Britain where different sports were followed by peasant and court. Many of these activities were the origins of our modern sports.

The next stage of development occurred in the great public schools at the start of the nineteenth century. Here boys adopted the old games, refining them into more formal and regular activities. On leaving school the old boys began to transport their love of games around Britain and the British Empire.

The Industrial Revolution changed the way people worked and lived and consequently had a major impact on sport. Most people were now living in towns and cities, with less space for sport, and sports had to be adapted to suit the new urban conditions. Changes in working patterns led to all people having more time for leisure and a more regular style of sport developed.

The final phase of development saw the emergence of physical education in state schools at the start of the twentieth century.

Exam themes

→ Development of popular recreation in the UK pre-1800

→ The games and festivals of pre-industrial Britain

→ The development of sport in the English public schools

→ The impact athleticism had on wider society

→ The spread of British sports around the world

→ The role of the universities in developing sport

→ Rational recreation in an urban industrial society

→ The need for the codification and organisation of sport in the nineteenth century

→ The development of PE in British state schools

Topic checklist

AS ○ A2 ●	AQA	EDEXCEL	OCR	WJEC
Sport before 1800		○	●	
Sport in the English public schools	○	○	●	○
The impact of athleticism on society	○	○	●	○
Sport after 1800 – the rational phase	○	○	●	○
The development of PE in British state schools 1870–1944	○	○	●	○

Sport before 1800

The historical development of sport moves through four main phases and questions will either focus on a particular period or ask you to compare developments between phases.

1	**Popular recreation**	fifteenth to seventeenth century
2	**Public school**	eighteenth to nineteenth century
3	**Rationalisation and industrialisation**	nineteenth century
4	**Twentieth century developments** (PE)	twentieth century

Overview of sport before 1800s

In the Middle Ages, the UK's population was almost totally rural. London (the only substantial town in the twelfth century) had a population of only 20,000. There were 30 'holy' days in a year (as well as Sundays) when sports could be played.

The population was split into two main groups: the gentry and the peasants.

For the gentry the amount of time available, economic and social advantage, and the need to demonstrate their military preparedness made the sporting activities of the ruling classes different from those of the peasants. Key sports were jousting for knights and sports such as real tennis that required sophisticated courts and equipment.

The time available for the peasants to play sport was often restricted to the holy days. They also had less access to resources and travel, so their recreations had to be localised and use ready-to-hand materials. Recreations changed through the year. In the winter mass, violent games such as mob football were played; in the summer gentler, more individual and athletic-type activities were followed. The games were often violent contests with few rules.

Take note

It is important that you get your dates right:

1600s seventeenth century	Pre-industrial
1700s eighteenth century	Pre- into industrial
1800s nineteenth century	Industrial
1900s twentieth century	Post-industrial
2000s twenty-first century	Technological

Checkpoint 1

Explain how real tennis was sophisticated in its make-up.

Examiner's secrets

Make sure you recognise the importance of combat sports and their link to the knights and war preparation.

Checkpoint 2

At what time of year were violent mob-type games usually played?

Take note

Pre-1800 characteristics of sport

P re
L ocalised
U ncoded
C ruel
I ndustrial
C ourtly/popular
R ural
O ccasional
W ager

Role of the Church ●●●

The year began with the spring fertility festivals, although some games took place as early as New Year's Day and Plough Monday (first Monday after Christmas). Most, however, focussed on Easter. Shrove Tuesday was a particularly popular day for violent mob games (football, tug of war and animal baiting), before the denials of Lent. May Day was often marked by games in which young men chased women, again concerned with rituals of fertility. Whitsuntide was the high point of the sporting year with much dancing and games. This was a slack time for agriculture, and crops and animals were left to grow! Summer games tended to be gentler – running, jumping and throwing contests. The church also provided space to play and would often offer patronage to games and festivals, perhaps providing prizes.

Checkpoint 3

Why were combat sports so popular in pre-industrial society?

The jargon

Holy day – a religious festival, which gave the people a day off from work. The usual Christian festivals and local saints days were often used for recreation.

Checkpoint 4

How did the agricultural year affect the time available for sport?

Exam questions   answers: page 98

Sport in the UK before 1800 was closely associated with the Church calendar of holy days and wakes.

1   Why were these days so important for the development of sport?

(6 minutes)

2   Outline the main characteristics of pre-industrial festival games.

(6 minutes)

Sport in the English public schools

In the public schools of the upper classes organised games began to appear, at first as spontaneous recreations and for the most part disapproved of by the teachers. However, as they became more developed it was recognised that educational objectives could be passed on through participation in games.

Sports became a feature of all public schools with team games forming the central core, particularly football and cricket (and rowing at the schools situated near a river). These games were physically strenuous, demanding and relied on cooperation and leadership – all characteristics that a gentleman needed to acquire.

Checkpoint 1

Why were games given so much importance in the public schools?

The three stages of development of the games cult

The change in attitude to sports and games in public schools during the nineteenth century is best viewed as a three-stage progression:

1 The barbarian phase 1790–1830
2 The Arnoldian/athleticism phase
3 The games cult and philistine copies.

The barbarian phase
During this period schools were unruly places, and there was a constant battle between staff and pupils for control. Boys would bring to school the games and recreations they had taken part in at home. These would have included mob games (various forms of football and stick and ball games) which were mainly spontaneous and very violent. Animal sports were also popular – either hunting or baiting/fighting sports.

The Arnoldian/athleticism phase
In 1827 Dr Thomas Arnold became headmaster of Rugby School, and he was to have an important influence on the reform of the public schools. Although Arnold's main concern was with the education and control of his pupils the programmes and rules he introduced had a parallel effect on the reform of games and sports in schools.

His main innovations were to introduce:

→ **The house system**, which neatly led to the formation of early sports team prefects who would organise the games and activities of the boys – the first administrators.
→ **Bounds**, whereby games and fights were confined to the school's grounds.
→ **Muscular Christianity** – the idea that there is a close link between Christianity and the concept of sportsmanship.
→ **Philosophy of character** – games were soon seen as a vehicle for developing character.

The games cult and philistine copies

The success of schools such as Rugby led to the cult of games spreading throughout the private education system. The Industrial Revolution was now in full swing, creating a new affluent middle class which provided a huge market for private education. Middle-class families wanted their sons to be educated as gentlemen and to service this need there was a huge growth of preparatory schools. The prominence for games and sports was further enhanced with the publication of the Clarendon Commission report in 1864. Its role was to investigate the management and programmes of the nine great public schools.

The Clarendon Committee 1864 ●●●

The Committee's main finding was that these schools instilled character in their pupils, many of whom went on to become influential leaders in all walks of life both in Britain and around the Empire. The Commission stated that the system of team games followed by these schools was the main developer of character. Football in particular was singled out as encouraging stamina, courage and the ability to withstand knocks.

Checkpoint 2

How did Arnold change the way sports were organised and controlled in the public schools?

The captain of the eleven; what a post is his in our school world; almost as hard as the Doctor's; requiring skill, gentleness and firmness, and I know not what other rare qualities.

Tom Brown's School Days

Checkpoint 3

Why was it difficult for schools to play each other at sport during the early nineteenth century?

Checkpoint 4

How did the Clarendon Commission promote the games cult?

Exam question   answer: page 98

What features of the nineteenth-century schools facilitated regular sports competition.   (8 minutes)

The impact of athleticism on society

The emergence of a modern form of sport through the public school system of the nineteenth century was to have a profound effect on the spread of sport throughout society, both in Britain and throughout the British Empire. It sowed the seeds of the rationalisation of sport, in which sports were codified and regulated by governing bodies, and the boys who left the schools spread the cult of manly games across the world.

Checkpoint 1

What is meant by the term 'sport followed the flag'?

If we ask what our Muscular Christianity has done – we point to the British Empire.

JGC Minchin, 1889

Take note

The Oxford and Cambridge Boat Race, created in 1829, is one of the oldest sporting events in the world.

Exploring the games ethic

The missionaries, ambassadors, generals and businessmen initially used games for their own recreation but then began to pass them onto the indigenous peoples of the colonies and other trading nations. The philosophy being to develop some of the moral characteristics that were so important to the English gentleman. Central to this philosophy were team games, these proved to be the perfect medium for transferring the favourable virtues that made up the games cult.

Through these sports the indigenous people could learn the basic tools of imperial command: courage, endurance, discipline, loyalty and obedience. Cricket supplied a new conception of chivalry that seemed to reflect exactly the national characteristics of Victorian England. Rugby and football promoted values more suited to imperialism: fearlessness and self-control. In summary, the games developed and promoted by the public schools could produce both the confidence to lead among the ex-pat British and the compulsion to follow among the indigenous people.

Imperialism was felt by most in Britain to be a very worthwhile, Christian activity. They were moralising and civilising the world – with sport an essential element of this. There were also more sound political reasons for the creation and maintenance of the Empire: trade, security, emigration, prestige and, in the case of Australia, somewhere to dump any criminals or social misfits.

Public school sport travels the world

An effective way of summarising this impact is CAT PUICCA.

C – colonial Many boys took up posts in the colonial service, helping to administer and govern the Empire's many colonies. They took with them their sporting kit. Initially they played among themselves but gradually introduced the sports and games to the indigenous populations.

A – army Another career for many boys was as commissioned officers in the armed forces. Initially the officers would use sports as a recreation to fill in long hours, but the social control and moral value on keeping the working-class soldiers occupied were not lost on them. This played an important part in spreading the cult still further.

T – teaching Many former pupils became teachers, especially in the new expanding preparatory and grammar schools. Often they simply repeated the programme of games and physical recreation they had followed in their schooldays. It was not unusual for sporty teachers to play for the school teams at the end of the nineteenth century.

P – patronage Supporting sporting events and competitions by providing funding for trophies or land for pitches (and in other ways) was another important role undertaken by old boys.

U – university This was a very important stage. Cambridge and Oxford chiefly gave young men further time and resources to pursue and refine sporting activities. One major problem though was the plethora of different rules for the various games. In order to allow all to play, compromise rules were required and this was the first step towards the rationalisation of sport.

I – industry Once they had finished school many boys returned to their fathers' factories and businesses. These were Arnold's 'philistines'. Their love of sport needed an outlet and soon clubs linked to these factories were set up. At first there were some social limits – only managers and office staff could join the teams – but gradually the lower classes were also admitted. Many current football teams – Stoke City, West Ham, Manchester United – were formed in this way.

C – Church Much of the boys' education was religion based, so it is not surprising that many boys took up careers in the Church. Muscular Christianity promoted the use of sport as a vehicle for teaching morals and Christian virtues. Many clergymen used it in its most practical form, encouraging sports and setting up teams both here and abroad. Again there are examples in modern football – Aston Villa, Everton and Wolverhampton Wanderers have Church origins.

C – clubs The first stage for many old boys was to form clubs so they could continue to play their games. The Old Etonians is a good example of this type of club, but many more were also formed.

A – administration When their playing days were over, many men joined and developed governing bodies for their sports, and helped to formulate national rules.

Checkpoint 2

Why were so many new schools built and opened in the second half of the nineteenth century?

Checkpoint 3

Why were the universities of Cambridge and Oxford known as the 'melting pots' of sports?

Exam question   answer: page 98

What role did Oxford and Cambridge play in the development of sport during the nineteenth century?   (8 minutes)

Sport after 1800 – the rational phase

The jargon

Codification – the creation and maintenance of rules.

Checkpoint 1

What effect did urbanisation and industrialisation have on sport during the nineteenth century?

Checkpoint 2

How did the half-day acts facilitate the development of sport at the end of the nineteenth century?

The phase referred to as the rationalisation of sport saw the codification and administration of sport. After the Industrial Revolution most people lived and worked in urban areas and the influence of the rural elements from the popular recreation era steadily declined. Modern sport is also urban sport.

Societal determinants – societal change that led to rational recreation

→ **Urbanisation** – Large population requiring recreative space and entertainment
→ **Industrialisation** – Factory system and machine time
→ **Work conditions** – Gradual increase in free time, Saturday half-day, Ten Hour Act, Early Closing Movement.
→ **Economics** – Capitalism and patronage, works teams – professional clubs.

Time for sport was governed by social class, and the working classes had to wait much longer for free time than the middle and upper classes. The development of transport allowed inter-town sport competitions and opened up the countryside. Urbanisation meant that only a few people could play, leading to spectatorism and inevitably professionalism. Rational sport became characterised by channelled aggression, stringent organisation, formal rules and regular play. The Factory Acts of the late nineteenth century finally gave working-class people more leisure time with most being given Saturday afternoons off work.

Working-class people tended to be drawn to sports that could make money – lack of leisure time meant that playing sport often meant the loss of wages, a situation few working people could afford. This led to sports teams in football and rugby paying players 'broken-time payments', a development that caused much ill feeling between the classes and led to a further division – a north–south divide (clubs in the north tended to be more open towards paying working-class players). Towards the end of the nineteenth century this led to the development of professionalism in many sports.

Initially fixtures among clubs were rather *ad hoc* affairs. Gentlemen's clubs would arrange fixtures on a day and date that suited both parties, and most of these amateur players had no constraints on when and where they could play. The rules played to were also rather informal – games could change at half-time from football rules to rugby rules. Generally the home team chose the particular rule and the away team provided the ball – but this did not always work in harmony.

As more and more teams became active, this *ad hoc* arrangement had to change. Clubs began to meet and form associations in order to make matches more regular and to reach a compromise over the rules of play. Such meetings ultimately led to the formation of national governing bodies in all major sports by the end of the nineteenth century.

The jargon

Broken time payments – clubs paid working-class players the wages they could not earn while playing.

Checkpoint 3

How had the relationship between spectators and performers changed by the end of the nineteenth century?

Checkpoint 4

What changes in sport led to the need for governing bodies at the end of the nineteenth century?

Examiner's secrets

You may be asked to compare the characteristics of popular and rational recreation. Draw a table and use the pneumonic PLUCI CROW as a start point. Look for opposites to summarise sport in the rational phase.

Exam question   answer: page 98

Explain the effect that both the transport and urban revolutions had on the organisation of rational sport at the start of the twentieth century.

(10 minutes)

The development of PE in British state schools

Modern PE grew from two main pathways: games from the public schools, which aimed to develop character and leadership, and physical training from elementary schools, devised to develop fitness and discipline. The 1870 Forster Act made education compulsory, but there was limited development of PE due to the lack of facilities and space.

Take note

Physical education developed through stages: drill → physical training → physical education.

Checkpoint 1

Why was there only a limited development of PE in state schools prior to 1870?

Take note

The 1870 Education Act set up Education Boards, funded in part through rates, to establish primary education.

Checkpoint 2

What role did Madame Bergman Osterberg play in the development of physical education in the UK?

Early forms of physical education

There were two main influences on this gymnastic development, stemming from two different European countries:

→ **German** – based on the work of Guts Muths and Friedrich Jahn
→ **Swedish** – based on the work of Per Henrik Ling.

It was the Swedish system of 'drill', inspired by Ling, that had the biggest impact on the development of physical education in Britain. Using the German system as his inspiration, Ling simplified the exercises and reduced the military bias, concentrating more on style and grace. He also paid respect to the classical tradition, emphasising the harmony between body and mind. Ling's system was adopted by many school boards in Britain – most importantly the London School Board, who appointed Madame Bergman Osterberg to oversee this implementation. She played a central role in the development of PE in Britain, establishing the first specialist teacher-training college at Dartford in 1895.

The model course

The first model course for physical education in schools was written by the War Office in 1902, prompted by the poor health of recruits for the Boer War. This syllabus was revised with a different focus in 1904–19, and a modern syllabus, taking the best of physical training and introducing PE as a subject in schools, was introduced in 1933. Developments during the Second World War led to an educational and more child-centred approach with the publication of *Moving and Growing* and *Planning the Programme*.

1870–1944

Key developments

→ nineteenth century – European roots *Ling and Guts Muths*

→ 1870 – Forster Education Act. *Made education compulsory for all children 5–13*

→ 1902 – Model course. *Compulsory military training in schools required to lay the foundations of military spirit in the nation*

→ 1904 – Education Board syllabus. *An attempt to reduce the military influence*

→ 1909 – Syllabus of Physical Training. *Written by Medical Board – emphasis on therapeutic gymnastics*

→ 1919 – Syllabus. *Reflecting the horrors of the Great War – introduced recreational and morale-boosting activities*

→ 1933 – Syllabus of Physical Training. *Last Board of Education syllabus split into two sections 5–11 years and 11–14 years*

→ 1944 – Education Act. *Made secondary education available to all children – rebuilding of schools after the blitz*

→ 1952 – *Moving and Growing. Ministry of Education advisory PE publication followed by* Planning the Programe (1954).

PE after 1945 ●●●

Post-war educational philosophy also led to a movement away from prescribed syllabuses and in 1952 the Ministry of Education published *Moving and Growing* and in 1954 *Planning the Programme*. All PE teachers received copies. These publications offered advice and suggestions rather than commands and represented the final move towards a child-centred approach to physical education.

Sport in the twentieth century ●●●

Several factors have affected the development of sport through the twentieth century. There was a steady move away from participation in sport to the phenomenon of watching sport, initially through spectatorism but increasingly through the media. Spectatorism generated money, which led to professionalism in virtually all sports. Many sports performers are now full-time paid entertainers.

Checkpoint 3

Who was responsible for writing the model course and what was the resulting bias?

Checkpoint 4

How did *Moving and Growing*, published in 1944, differ from earlier syllabuses?

Examiner's secrets

There is a lot to cover here, make sure you have a good knowledge of the key developments and don't forget to write about the influence of war.

Exam question   answer: page 99

How did war influence the early development of physical education in British state schools at the beginning of the twentieth century?   (8 minutes)

Answers
Historical study of physical education and sport

Sport before 1800

Checkpoints

1 Real tennis was a sophisticated game. It required a purpose-built court, the equipment was handmade and had no other use than playing tennis. The scoring system of the game required education and a basic knowledge of arithmetic.
2 Mob-type games tended to be played during the winter – the need to move and to keep warm with no problems over using the field as pitches.
3 Combat sports were popular in pre-industrial society because of the need to be fit for war. They also offered a chance for gambling and entertainment and were easily accessible for all classes.
4 The agricultural year governed how much spare time the people had, spring and autumn were busy times with little time for sports, whereas in winter and summer there was more time.

Exam questions

1 Holy days and wakes were important for the development of sport because these were the only days free from work when large groups of the community could come together. Patronage by the church was in the form of providing land for games and prizes.
2 The main characteristics of pre-industrial festival games were the use of large spaces and games were rural activities. They were only played once a year/occasionally, were only played in a particular place and with no transport it meant that games were localised. Games had few rules, said to be uncoded, often violent, involving large numbers of participants, there was a loose distinction between participants and spectators.

Sport in the English public schools

Checkpoints

1 Games were given much importance in the public school system. Games developed character and reinforced many of the values, such as leadership and honour, that a gentlemen was meant to possess, they were also an effective means of social control.
2 Arnold gave responsibility of organising sports to the prefects and sixth-formers.
3 The difficulty for schools wanting to play each other was that transport was still a limiting factor, so the main focus for competition was house matches.
4 The Clarendon Commission reported that the best schools in the UK all had extensive systems of school sport.

Exam question

Features of the nineteenth-century schools that facilitated regular sports competition were:
The house structure of the boarding schools gave a natural focus for competition, there was also support from headmasters and they allowed time after lessons for the boys to play. Control by the upper school gave a certain degree of peer pressure.

The impact of athleticism on society

Checkpoints

1 In sport the term 'followed the flag' refers to the way in which sports that originated in Britain quickly spread across the rest of the world, especially where the British colonial influence was strong.
2 Many new schools were built and opened in the second half of the nineteenth century because the expanding middle class meant that there was a demand to send sons and daughters to private or preparatory schools.
3 Cambridge and Oxford were known as the 'melting pots' of sport. Melting pot refers to the fact that undergraduates brought various rules of games from the many public schools to the universities which were the first place where an attempt at creating compromise rules occurred.

Exam question

Oxford and Cambridge university acted as a melting pot for the mixing of the numerous versions of sports rules arriving from the schools.

Sport after 1800 – the rational phase

Checkpoints

1 Urbanisation meant a lack of space for sport, and industrialisation changed the calendar and meant there was less time for sport.
2 The half-day acts gave working-class people to time to take up sport, so increasing the participation rates.
3 There was now a clear distinction between spectators and players, pitch markings and stadia now kept them well apart.
4 By the end of the nineteenth century transport had developed which allowed teams and individuals to travel, so there was now a need for national sets of rules and bodies to organise fixtures and competitions.

Exam question

The effects that the transport and urban revolutions had on the organisation of rational sport at the start of the twentieth century are:
The transport revolution meant that teams could travel to play one another, which led to a need for national sets of rules and the formation of governing bodies, this also meant that national leagues and competitions could be set up. Urbanisation meant there was less space to play sport and that pitches had to be formalised. It also led to the rise in spectatorism since large numbers could no longer play sport.

The development of PE in British state schools 1870–1944

Checkpoints

1 There was limited development of PE in state schools prior to 1870 because schooling was not compulsory before 1870, so very few working-class children would have attended.

2 Madame Bergman Osterberg played a central role in the development of PE in Britain. She introduced a system of Swedish drill to schools in London and set up the first training college for PE teachers.

3 The War Office produced the model course and this resulted in a very military approach, treating pupils as little soldiers.

4 *Moving and Growing* only offered guidance and suggestions, there was no compulsion or prescription.

Exam question

The need for a fit and obedient working-class army affected the scope and provision of PE, the failings of the Boer War led to the introduction of the model course written and produced by the War Office, this course was taught by NCOs. The First World War led to a re-emphasis of drill, though the role that sports and games had played in the convalescence camps was acknowledged. The Second World War led to a more child-centred approach mirroring change in military tactics and also the rebuilding of schools with sports facilities.

Revision checklist
Historical study of physical education and sport

By the end of this chapter you should be able to:

		Confident	Not confident.
1	Outline the development of popular recreation in the UK pre-1800	Confident ✓	Not confident. **Revise** pages 88–89
2	Explain the importance of combat sports and their link to the knights and war preparation in pre-industrial society	Confident ✓	Not confident. **Revise** pages 88–89
3	Give examples of and describe the games and festivals of pre-industrial Britain	Confident	Not confident. **Revise** pages 88–89
4	Trace the development of sport in the English public schools	Confident	Not confident. **Revise** pages 90–91
5	Explain the role of the universities in developing sport during the nineteenth century	Confident	Not confident. **Revise** pages 90–91
6	Describe the effect urbanisation and industrialisation had on sport during the nineteenth century	Confident	Not confident. **Revise** pages 92–95
7	Describe how the half-day acts facilitated the development of sport at the end of the nineteenth century	Confident	Not confident. **Revise** pages 92–95
8	Explain the changes in sport that led to the need for governing bodies at the end of the nineteenth century	Confident	Not confident. **Revise** pages 92–95
9	Discuss how physical education developed through stages: drill → physical training → physical education	Confident	Not confident. **Revise** pages 96–97
10	Explain the structure of and need for the model course introduced in 1902	Confident	Not confident. **Revise** pages 96–97

The comparative study of global sporting systems

The key to understanding comparative study is to recognise that sport reflects the culture in which it is being played. Socio-cultural difference will have an effect on the way sport is organised and provided, and opportunities to participate may differ between cultures. Some examination boards require students to undertake a comparative analysis of sport using the UK as the base culture so it may be worth reviewing the material covered in the seventh chapter of this guide.

For each culture we will investigate the socio-cultural background then trace the historical development of sport and discuss how sport is organised now. We also need to investigate the role that physical education and school sport play in the society and contrast élite and mass sport.

Exam themes

→ Overview of sport in the USA

→ The administration of sport in the USA

→ Historical development of sport and PE in the USA

→ Mass participation and élite sport in the USA

→ Culture and background of Australian sport

→ Overview of sport in Australia

→ Historical development of Australian sport and PE

→ The administration of sport in Australia

→ School and college sport in Australia

→ Mass participation and élite sport in Australia

→ Culture and background of sport in France

→ Overview of sport in France

→ Historical development of sport and PE in France

→ The administration of sport in France

→ Mass participation and élite sport in France

Topic checklist

AS ○ A2 ●	AQA	EDEXCEL	OCR	WJEC
Sport in North American cultures	●	●	●	●
Administration of sport in North American cultures	●	●	●	●
Mass participation and élite sport in the USA	●	●	●	●
Sport in New World culture – Australia		●	●	●
Administration of sport in Australia		●	●	●
Mass participation and élite sport in Australia		●	●	●
Sport in France	●		●	●
PE and school sport in France	●		●	●
Mass participation and élite sport in France	●		●	●

Sport in North American cultures

America's major sports are not really played anywhere else in the world – this is a good example of sport reflecting the culture of a society. America's history and self-belief have established a sports system where it can hold 'world championships' in American football, baseball, basketball and ice hockey in which only American teams compete.

Overview ●●●

→ Sports most technically advanced in world
→ Sports stars are the richest in the world
→ Sports-mad public – large audiences
→ World champions in a number of sports
→ Americanisation spreading throughout global sport.

America's sports tend to be high scoring and action-packed to maximise their entertainment value. They reflect American culture in that the aim is to win – the win ethic, or Lombardian ethic, is what drives all American people and this fuels the 'American Dream' (this idea of rags to riches success is best personified in the 'Rocky' films, where a nobody becomes world champion overnight).

The commercial aspect of American sport makes it unique. Every level, from professional national teams to the local high-school football team, is run as a business. The influence of television is total and most sports rely on the money generated through television deals and advertising revenue. Sports stars in America are millionaires – indeed, most professional teams will have a number of players on multi-million-dollar contracts. Many stars, like Michael Jordan, make even more money through sponsorship deals and endorsements.

The historical development of sport in North American cultures ●●●

	Historical phase of development	Sports phase of development	Sports example
1	Heritage of ancient civilisations	Ancient Games	Baggataway/ Lacrosse
2	Arrival of the Europeans	Arrival of the Europeans	Baseball
3	Rationalisation phase	Rationalisation phase	American football
4	New image and isolation and ethnic melting pot	New image and isolation	Basketball
5	Superpower	Sport the commodity	Extreme sports

Checkpoint 1

Explain how the rags to riches ideal can be achieved through sport in the USA.

Checkpoint 2

What is meant by the term 'endorsement'?

Checkpoint 3

Sport in the USA is dominated by the private sector, what forms of funding are available to US sports?

The jargon

Lombardian ethic – named after the famous Green Bay Packers' most successful coach Vince Lombardi, who developed the idea that winning is the most important thing.

The jargon

American Dream – the idea that in the USA anyone can rise from rags to riches.

The USA was once a colony of Great Britain, but this link was severed early in the country's development and for many years the USA developed in planned isolation from the rest of the world, and in particular Europe. During this period many of America's sports were adapted from old European games to suit America's new image. In sports such as football and hockey a more robust, glamorous version has developed and distinctive American sports (such as basketball) were invented on American soil. So closely did these sports mirror American society that they have never really developed away from America's shores.

The commercial nature of American sport ●●●

Every level from professional teams to the local high-school football team is run as a business. The influence of the media is total and most of the national sports in North America rely on money generated through television deals and advertising revenue. Television has so much power in American sport that it can even dictate a sport's rules. American football, for example, has evolved into a game with many stoppages so that TV companies can screen advertisements every five minutes. Sports stars in America become millionaires from their playing contracts and can earn much more money through sponsorship deals and endorsements.

This commercial nature does mean though that sport in America is extremely élitist and there are very few amateur clubs or opportunities for people of lower ability to access sport. Nearly all of America's sports clubs are based in educational establishments such as schools and colleges or professional enterprises. This means that for most Americans sport is something you watch on television and is not something most people play after leaving school.

Checkpoint 4

How does American football reflect the culture of the USA?

The jargon

Endorsement – where a sports star is paid to put their name into the sale of a product or a commodity.

Exam question   answer: page 120

Give historical and cultural reasons to explain the fact that the USA holds 'world championships' in sports which only American teams compete in.

(8 minutes)

Administration of sport in North American cultures

There is a decentralised administration with autonomous governing bodies in North American culture. There are a small number of powerful professional sports with considerable public support, run as profit-making businesses through the franchise system. There is much commercial sponsorship and major media influence – the private sector is the main source of funding. Lomabardian 'win at all costs' ethic dominates through all American sport and is reflected in the link between professionalism and capitalism, although there is a strong and growing counter-culture movement linking the rise of lifetime sport and eco sport. The college system acts as a sponsored nursery for professional and Olympic sport. There are limited opportunities for amateur sport and few public facilities.

School and college sport

School and college sport in the USA is unique, in sparsely populated areas or less well-off areas, where long distances must be travelled to watch one of the professional National League teams, the school or college team becomes a substitute for community attention.

Sport in high schools – key points

→ High-school sports form a link between education and professional sports
→ High-school sports are a microcosm of professional games
→ Most high schools possess lavish facilities for sports
→ School sports are followed by community
→ School sports are funded by boosters.

High-school sports link the education system and professional sports industries.

High-school Team

↓

College Scholarship

↓

Draft

↓

Professional League

Checkpoint 1

What is meant by the term 'autonomous'?

The jargon

Booster clubs. Community clubs made up of old boys and local businessmen that help support financially school and college teams.

The jargon

Draft system. The system where professional teams select the best college players once a year.

Checkpoint 2

What does Title IX legislate against?

Checkpoint 3

What role do booster clubs play in the financing and promotion of school and college sport?

School and college sport is the main route to a career in sport and a unique feature is recruitment through school–college–professional leagues, but the system is very elitist with only 3 per cent moving from school to college teams and in basketball only 1 in 10,000 get into draft. Coaches and scouts working for the college visit high schools across the country, identifying and attempting to recruit players to come and play for their team. To attract players they emphasise the quality of their facilities, the chances of playing in a successful team and therefore a better chance of making the 'draft' – and, of course, the 'athletic scholarship'.

The draft system ●●○

This acts as the bridge between the college system and professional leagues. The draft system, together with salary capping, ensures that teams are simply not able to buy their way to success.

In the draft system, teams in each of the major professional sports are ranked at the end of each season, as are the outstanding college players likely to arouse the interest of professional clubs. The lowest-ranked club has the first choice of the highest-ranked player so that, theoretically at least, some form of parity is maintained.

Intramural sport does exist and is where players of a lower standard play for fun. It is very low profile and often occurs late at night after the college teams have finished training.

The jargon

Athletic scholarships. Grant-in-aid to help cover tuition fees and board.

Checkpoint 4

How does the draft system attempt to reflect the American ideal of the land of opportunity?

Exam question   answer: page 120

Suggest reasons for the huge community interest and support for high-school sport in the USA.   (8 minutes)

Mass participation and élite sport in the USA

American sport has not evolved a sports club system similar to that in northern Europe. Sport tends to be focussed on high school, college and professional franchises. There is only limited opportunity outside these spheres to participate in sports.

Mass participation ●●●

Urban parks and other open spaces do offer Americans the chance to jog, skate and play touch football or softball, but generally there is little public-sector sport provision.

One exception is 'little league' sport, club leagues for children under 10 run in a number of different sports – Pop Warner football, Pee Wee Baseball and Biddy Basketball are examples.

Teams are run by parents and compete in structured league competitions that mirror the professional leagues, with conferences, play-offs and 'superbowls'. The main emphasis is on winning and this has led to some criticism; however, most Americans support the system because they feel that it helps reinforce in children the American way of life. The current USA President is a former little league baseball player – which has led to the motto: 'from little league to White House'.

As we have previously discussed, the ethic of sport in America has been replaced by spectatorism with most Americans happy to watch élite performers play. There has been a recent move towards lifetime sport, mainly to counter problems over increasing levels of obesity among the American population. This move towards participation has been readily taken up by older Americans with most areas now holding 'golden Olympics'.

Alternative and wilderness sports ●●●

The National Parks Service created in 1916 reflected the aim of America as the land of the free. The combination of cars and a wilderness that is easily accessible gives most Americans the chance to experience the frontier spirit. One of the areas that has increased in popularity is the so-called eco sport. Activities such as skiing, backpacking, white-water rafting and mountain biking have boomed in recent years. These activities are part of a counter-culture, an escape from the élite 'win ethic' culture of most American sport.

Checkpoint 1

Explain what is meant by the term 'professional franchise'.

The jargon

Lifetime sport. A sport that can be played throughout a person's life.

Checkpoint 2

How does little league sport mirror the professional sports scene of the USA?

The jargon

Title IX. Made law in 1972 this laid down rights of this access to sport for women and girls on an equal basis to men. Equal opportunity had to be provided for facilities, coaching and financial support. If an institution that received federal money failed to provide equal opportunity, then these monies would be withheld.

Many American children also attend summer camps, these residential activity camps are usually sited well away from cities and towns and often concentrate on outdoor sports and activities. There are thousands of these camps across the states catering for all pockets and tastes.

Private camps	Very exclusive and expensive, these are often very specialised catering for specific sports or interests. The more traditional camps still focus on developing a sense of frontier spirit among camp attendees
Charity and church camps	Here costs are subsidised due to sponsorship from church or charity groups, these camps tend to offer a range of outdoor activities
State camps	Here the state government pays for under-privileged children to attend a summer camp

Professional and élite sport ●●●

Sport in the USA is run through a decentralised system of autonomous governing bodies with little state or federal intervention. A number of powerful professional sports enjoy considerable support from the American public. These sports are run on a franchise basis and are very commercially oriented, with the main priority of all clubs to make a profit.

The private sector dominates American sport; there is very little voluntary or public-sector provision. Sport relies on gate receipts, media fees and, increasingly, commercial sponsorship.

Checkpoint 3

Explain what is meant by the term 'counter-culture'?

The jargon

Eco sport. Recreational activities with little organisation and natural in focus.

The jargon

Franchise. A business agreement set up to maximise profit.

Checkpoint 4

Explain the role the media play in sport in the USA.

Exam question   answer: page 120

Suggest why the ethic of mass participation may not sit comfortably in the culture of the USA.   (7 minutes)

Sport in New World culture – Australia

Australia has a comparatively small population, yet enjoys an extraordinary degree of success on the sports field and there are few sporting events in which Australia does not excel. Statistics show that Australia gains more Olympic gold medals than any other nation.

Cultural background

Australia's is a 'young' country, in terms of both its culture and its population – nearly half its population is under the age of 30 (in the UK 50 per cent of the population are over the age of 50).

It has a relatively small population of only 18 million, and so one would think that it was a sparsely populated country. In some ways this is true but Australia is also a land of contradictions and is in fact one of the most urbanised populations – 85 per cent of the population live in only 3.3 per cent of the nation's land area.

Australia's people

The original inhabitants of Australia, the Aboriginal people, are one of the oldest civilisations in the world. They arrived in Australia during the Ice Age when Australia was connected to Asia via land bridges. But as it moved away from the Asian continent, Australia and its inhabitants were isolated for several thousands of years, until in the eighteenth century European explorers discovered Terra Australis Incognita ('the unknown southern land').

Historical development

The British established a colony in Australia in 1788. A fleet of 11 vessels containing 736 convicted criminals, a governor, some officials and an escort of Royal Marines founded the colony on the eastern coast of Australia in what later became New South Wales. This was the first European settlement of any kind in Australia, an area that was as yet little known about in Europe.

Checkpoint 1

Explain how having a 'youthful' population is an advantage in terms of international sporting success.

Transportation was an important part of the British penal system. Convicts had, before this time, been sent to America but now the American Revolution and independence meant that this country could no longer be used. By 1852, 160,000 convicts had been sent to Australia. After the establishment of the first colony, many 'free settlers' also left Britain for Australia. This immigration gained pace in the 1850s when gold was discovered in many areas of south-west Australia. By 1861 there were over 1 million white Australians (compare this with the native population – in 1887 there were only 750,000 Aborigines).

After the First World War, Britain's hold on the colonies began to dwindle and the Balfour Declaration of 1926 and the Statute of Westminster, 1931, conceded control to the colonies and led to the recognition of Australia's states as governments in their own right.

Geography and culture ●●●

Though a vast and diverse country, as we have mentioned above, the majority of the Australian people live on the low-lying coastal plains running around the south and east coast. This again has a positive impact on sport, these areas experience a temperate climate which is favourable for sport in the outdoors. It also means that a large percentage of the Australian population lives very close to the thousands of miles of beach and coastline – a free and accessible natural facility for a range of sports. The size and diversity of the country also means that there are numerous opportunities for a vast range of sports from skiing to surfing.

Checkpoint 2

How did the transportation system aid the development of Australia?

Checkpoint 3

How is Australia's colonial history reflected in the sports they play?

Checkpoint 4

How does being a member of the Commonwealth maintain the link between Australia and the UK?

Exam question   answer: page 120

Explain the popularity of outdoor sport and activities both in Australian schools and communities.   (8 minutes)

Administration of sport in Australia

Australia consists of a number of self-governing states and two areas that have territorial status. The country is governed under a federal system similar to the one that operates in the USA, the main difference being that Australia has maintained its commonwealth status and consequently the British queen is still its head of state. The system of administration is decentralised.

Administration of sport ●●●

The administration and organisation of sport and recreation in Australia follows this decentralised system, with each state and territory having a department responsible for sport and recreation and its own élite academy of sport. There is, however, another example of a compromise, with a powerful centralising effect from the federally funded Australian Sports Commission and its sports institute network.

Australia is certainly a sports obsessed nation with over 120 national sporting organisations and it is estimated that around six and a half million people, around a third of the population, are registered members of a sporting club.

The role of the Commonwealth government

The Commonwealth or federal government of Australia funds and develops sport and physical activity through the Australian Sports Commission. It also actively supports and funds the hosting of international sports events such as the 2000 Sydney Olympic and Paralympic Games

The role of the state government

There are six separate state governments in Australia and they all take an active role in the promotion and coordination of sport, physical education and active recreation. It is the state sport and recreation department, funded directly by government, that are responsible for implementing Active Australia programmes in their state. Each state also has their own policies and programmes that support both élite sport and mass participation.

The role of local government

Again this level of government plays an important role in delivering the Active Australia programmes. Local government is in the best position to assist services and distribute funds in the best interests of community groups.

The Australian Sports Commission has three main objectives:

1 To develop and maintain an effective national sports infrastructure.
2 To improve participation by Australians in quality sports activities.
3 To encourage excellence in sports performance by Australians.

Checkpoint 1

What is meant by the term 'federal' in the context of governance?

Example

The state of Victoria, for example, has established a dynamic Active for Life strategy, with its slogan 'Just find thirty minutes a day'.

The jargon

Australian Sports Commission. Set up in 1885 by the federal government, this is the body responsible for increasing participation and developing sports excellence in Australia.

Each state has its own sport and recreation department which are responsible for promoting sports participation in their own state. All states also have their own dynamic élite sports programme focused around an Institute of Sport.

PE and school provision ●●●

Physical education is compulsory in all Australian schools, although again there is variation in content and scheduling across the states. The education department in each state is responsible for all educational matters, though in the case of physical education and school sport they will often work closely with the state's department of sport and recreation.

Two programmes dominate sport for young people in Australia.

The Victoria Model

→ 100 minutes of PE a week compulsory.
→ 100 minutes of sport education a week compulsory.
→ All school teams must play in school time.
→ State department runs, funds and organises inter-school sport.

Fundamental Motor Skills Programme

→ Identification of key motor skills for adult sports.
→ Fair go for all.
→ Every primary school teacher in Victoria receives a copy.
→ Government schools can access further training free of charge.

Aussie sport programme ●●●

Developed by ASC and set up in 1986 the Aussie Sport programme was designed to overcome the lack of games skills and to increase participation in sport by school-aged children.

Programmes were run at weekends/out of school hours but used school facilities. The key was the introduction of 'mini' games – modified versions of adult games.

Examples of Aussie sport programmes include:

→ Netta netball
→ Minky hockey
→ Kick-A-Roo soccer
→ Auskick Aussie Rules.

Checkpoint 2

How does the administration of Australia's sport follow a decentralised system?

Checkpoint 3

Who is responsible for the structure and content of PE programmes in Australia?

Checkpoint 4

Explain the aim of the Fundamental Motor Skills Programme.

Exam question   answer: page 121

A unique feature of Australian schools is the provision of Sport Education Programmes (SEPEP) within the curriculum. Explain the structure and philosophy of the Sport Education Programme.   (9 minutes)

Mass participation and élite sport in Australia

Federal government figures suggest that 90 per cent of the Australian population actively participates in sports activities and there are 6.5 million registered players in Australia affiliated to over 30,000 sports clubs. This national framework, issued by the ASC, requires each state government's recreation department to set up and run programmes and campaigns that follow the guidelines and aims set out in the Active Australia policy document.

Mass participation

Active Australia is about promoting healthy lifestyles through participation in regular physical activity. Launched in 1997, Active Australia involves a nationwide network of schools and sport, and recreation and fitness clubs with links to federal, state and local government.

The programme focusses on two main areas:

→ Encouraging people to be more physically active.
→ Working to improve the places where people can be active.

The state departments of sport and recreation are involved in the actual delivery of Active Australia and where appropriate ensure that state-funded programmes share the same objectives.

Outdoor and adventure activities

Australia has a great range of areas of outstanding natural beauty and its modern integrated transport system makes the outback accessible to all Australians, many of whom make use of it at weekends and holidays. The other main natural resource is the extensive coastline, especially around the main population centres in the south-east. The beach and coast remain the most important recreational facility and related sports and activities such as surfing, fishing and boating are extremely popular.

Professional and élite sport

Australia followed Britain in its reluctance to accept professionalism in sport – even now, few Australian sports have totally embraced full-time professional status. Many Australian sports stars ply their trade on foreign shores, where the level of reward and chance of exposure is greater. The big two Australian sports – Australian rules football and rugby league – are both fully professional and supported by large audiences (both live and on television), commercial and sponsorship funding, as well as public funding, in the system of state and national sports academies. Professional sports tend to be administered by a hybrid system of British-style governing bodies operating through American-style franchise agreements.

Checkpoint 1

Outline the aims of the Active Australia programme.

Example

The Australian Sports Commission promotes active recreation for older members of its population through the Mature Age Sport Programme.

Checkpoint 2

Can you identify the natural and cultural advantages Australia may have over the UK in terms of sports participation?

Checkpoint 3

What geographical factors may limit the scope of professional sport in Australia?

It is in Olympic sport that the Australian system excels. Their preparation of athletes is now being copied by many other nations, including the UK. The formation of the Australian Institute of Sport (AIS) in 1981 was a significant move in terms of the nurturing of sports talent and government involvement in sports administration. The lead-up to the formation of the AIS followed a pattern similar to the one that occurred in France at the same time – failure at the 1976 Montreal Olympics led to a national outcry and spurred the federal government to fund and reorganise élite sport.

The Australian Institute of Sport ●●●

Possibly the best centre for élite athlete preparation in the world, this network of sports academies provides Australia's top performers with the best support. The AIS is funded 95 per cent from federal funds and 5 per cent from commercial sponsorship, with Kellogg's currently a major sponsor. Top athletes receive scholarships to attend the AIS – 500 full-time and 270 visiting scholarships are available each year.

The AIS is not simply one centre. Its main base is in the federal capital of Canberra but due to the vastness of Australia it runs a decentralised programme of outreach centres in each state's capital city.

Examiner's secrets

The institute system is a unique feature of sport in Australia and is a very popular topic for examiners to ask questions about.

Checkpoint 4

How does the structure of the AIS reflect the decentralising factors of the separate states in Australia?

The structure of Australian sport

Australian
Institute of Sport

State institutes

Club sport

Sepep and sport

Sports search

Aussie sport

Fundamental motor skills

Exam question   answer: page 121

Describe some of the strategies that Australia has used in an attempt to establish Olympic success.   (10 minutes)

Sport in France

France is geographically three times the size of the UK but has a very similar population and similar history and heritage. It therefore provides an interesting comparative analysis.

Cultural background

The differences in geography mean that France has a more rural culture and a lot more space – naturally this is reflected in the sports and pastimes that dominate French society. Over the last 20 years the French government has placed a lot of emphasis and funding on developing élite sports squads, which have performed at the Olympics and other global games. At the 1996 Olympics France won 15 gold medals and gained fourth place on the overall medal table; in 1998 the French soccer team became world champions.

The idea of international sport originated in France, when Pierre de Coubertin established the modern Olympic Games in 1896. As a young man, de Coubertin had witnessed the general apathy of the French population towards sports and blamed much of this failing to the gymnastic type of approach to sport that had developed.

He visited schools in England and was greatly impressed with their many football, cricket, track and rowing competitions. He saw a link between athletic sport and the perfect education for a country's young people. De Coubertin believed that these activities were the source of physical vigour and moral discipline that had enabled the British to rule such an enormous empire. He returned to France determined to propagate such activities in France and so raise the status of the French in international affairs. Hence France now competes on a world level in sports such as rugby, football and athletics.

Administration of French sport ●●●

French sport is centrally organised, with the French government and public sector taking a central role in the control and funding of sport. France has a centralised government and this model of control also covers sport and recreation. The Department of Youth and Sport controls French sport at all levels.

Although the club remains the basic unit, the key to the French approach is the federation – like UK governing bodies. However, these bodies are answerable to the Minister for Youth and Sport. The élite

Checkpoint 1

What types of sports suit France's rural nature?

Checkpoint 2

Explain what is meant by the term 'centralised' in terms of administration.

network is very much 'Top-down' with much government/central control. The National Olympic Committee is also answerable to the Ministry and there is considerable state support for élite sports centres and athletes. Poor results at the 1960 Rome Olympics dented national pride and prestige and the French President de Gaulle was very disappointed. He was determined to use sport as a form of nation building and as a tool to revitalise the French spirit. State aid was granted to improve facilities and administration support as part of a centralised approach. A National Institute of Sport (INSEP – see below) was established and a national plan for sport was put in place.

The structure of French sport resembles a pyramid

INSEP

CREPS

Sports study sections

UNSS sport

French sport also receives financial support from the national lottery – Le Lotto – importantly 30 per cent of the money generated is allocated to a national fund for the development of sport. This money is used chiefly to help the introduction of more sport in school and to assist advances in sports technology, medicine and coaching.

The jargon

National plan. Programme aimed at providing the whole French population with access to sports facilities.

Did you know

France restructured its administration of sport after poor results at the 1960 Rome Olympics.

Checkpoint 3

What role did President de Gaulle believe sporting success could bring to France?

The jargon

CREPS (Centre d'Education Populaire et de Sports) – regional centres of excellence that provide support for potential élite performers.

Checkpoint 4

How is the position of Sports Minister in France different from that in the UK?

Exam question   answer: page 121

Discuss the reasons behind the French government's support of sport at all levels.   (7 minutes)

PE and school sport in France

Physical education is currently controlled by the Department of Youth and Sport, mirroring the centralised system of control, and there is a true national curriculum and one that all schools are required to teach.

PE and sport in primary schools

At primary school level the 'tier temps pedagogique' programme divides up the primary curriculum into three equal parts: social, academic and physical. In theory this should result in primary schools offering six hours of physical education per week. However, there is a lack of supervision to enforce this requirement and, just as in the UK, the lack of facilities and suitably trained teachers further inhibits this programme. There is provision for extracurricular sport at primary level in the federal organisation Union Sportive de l'Enseignement Primaire (USEP – Primary Schools Sports Union). This organisation aims to promote sport at the primary level and sets up links with local clubs.

The other main focus of physical activity at primary level is the system of transplant classes. These are outdoor experiences that occur as part of the school curriculum. There are three main focusses, with ski class, sea class and countryside class – ski class being the most popular. The general pattern is that children are transplanted as a class to the natural environment for a week. In the mornings they follow normal lessons and in the afternoons they can take part in a range of outdoor activities.

PE and sport in secondary schools

The secondary school curriculum is prescribed by the official instructions called 'la programmation', this states the time allocation for each subject and also stipulates what should be taught. In theory all secondary schools should offer three hours of physical education per week, though again lack of facilities and pressure to fit in other subjects can restrict this. Physical education is a compulsory element of the baccalauréat.

It is now acknowledged that sporting objectives can be best achieved through sports afternoons coordinated by another federal body, the Union National du Sport Scolaire (UNSS – National Union of School Sport).

Checkpoint 1

Explain the 'tier temps pedagogique' programme.

The jargon

Tier temps pedagogique. 'A third time programme', where primary schools are required to teach six hours of physical education a week.

Checkpoint 2

What are the three types of transplant classes?

Sports afternoons

These are considered an official part of the school curriculum and most schools have no lessons on a Wednesday afternoon. The emphasis here is on playing sport and a clear pyramid of standard is apparent. Again there is central control of this feature: USEP and UNSS are given overall control, with regional federations running localised events. The system gives all schools an equal chance of participating in school sport. Schools receive support and funding to enable them to participate. There is some conflict in that, because the system is aimed at mass participation, the level of performance is low, and better performers will tend to gravitate towards local clubs who also tend to play junior fixtures on a Wednesday afternoon.

Sports study sections – Les sections sport-etudes ●●●

These are regional centres for teaching and training of élite young sports performers. They are structured to respond to the sporting needs of the élite, those who have already proved themselves in a particular sport, and – equally importantly – their academic study.

In order to enter these sections, which are attached to normal secondary schools, students must have reached a high standard in their sport, passed various medical tests and have attained a reasonable level of academic progress.

The students face a very demanding schedule. They cover the same academic programme as normal students and then have 10–15 hours of sports coaching each week.

Checkpoint 3

Discuss the conflict better school-age performers have on Wednesday afternoons.

The jargon

USEP. Union of Primary School Sport, responsible for coordinating Wednesday afternoon sport in *primary* schools.

The jargon

UNSS. National Union of School Sport, responsible for coordinating Wednesday afternoon sport in *secondary* schools.

Checkpoint 4

What is the role of the sports study sections?

Exam question   answer: pages 121–122

Identify examples of central control within the French education system.

(7 minutes)

Mass participation and élite sport in France

Well over six million people belong to French sporting clubs and sports such as tennis are extremely popular. Over four million French people ski on a regular basis.

Once again the government and centralised system of France has had an impact on the provision of sports and recreational facilities. A result of de Gaulle's plan was a concerted effort by national and local authorities to improve local facilities. This means that most urban areas have swimming pools and municipal sports centres.

Promoting mass participation in France

Access to leisure and physical recreation is also enhanced through state support for children's skiing and sailing trips and subsidised holidays for lower-income families. Sport Pour Tous was set up by the French government to try to promote mass physical recreation. It is similar to the UK's Sport for All campaign in both structure and philosophy.

The aim of the national plan was to provide enough sports equipment and facilities to meet the needs of the whole population. However, due to budget restraints, this has been achieved only in the building of swimming pools.

Mass participation in France tends to have a health bias, with the Department of Youth and Sport keen to play a major role in developing the health and fitness of the French population. One of the key slogans used is 'Sportez-vous bien' which means 'Play sport to keep fit.'

'Le plein air' – the outdoors – is an important element in French culture. France's natural resources are much in evidence and campaigns, such as 'le plein air', and rustic simplicity are central to French culture. Outdoor pursuits achieve the dual functions of possible medals and mass participation.

Professional and élite sport

Over the last 30 years France has consistently been ranked as one of the top Olympic nations. Much of this new-found success resulted from de Gaulle's vision for a new France after the Second World War.

Checkpoint 1

How does the transplant class system in French schools help promote mass participation?

Checkpoint 2

What was the purpose of the national plan?

Checkpoint 3

Explain why the topography and culture of France is suited to the ideal of 'rustic simplicity'.

President de Gaulle set in motion a review and then an overhaul of the sporting system. The control of sport was brought under government influence and now the Minister for Sport, working within the State Department of Youth Sport, has total control of all French sport, including élite preparation and professional organisations.

The government has developed a sound sporting infrastructure that is now paying dividends. A great deal of funding is directed towards sport at all levels but a large proportion is allocated to training élite athletes at a number of national centres. Support for sport occurs at all levels – state, regional and local, creating a clear pyramid structure. All organisations in France work to the same agenda and there is much cooperation.

The state pays for a great many coaches and administration staff, ensuring that they can concentrate all their time and energy on preparing France's top performers.

The route to excellence begins at school, where the programmes of physical education and sports afternoons are used to encourage young people into sport. Those who show promise are channelled towards specialist centres called sports study sections.

At INSEP 850 high-level athletes of the institute are presented with all facilities to help them succeed in their athletic and scholarly or professional goals. This means working in close collaboration with universities and institutions.

The jargon

Sport pour tous. A national scheme of mass participation.

The jargon

INSEP (Institute National Du Sport et de L'Education Physique) was founded in 1976 on the outskirts of Paris to provide training and preparation for France's élite athletes.

Checkpoint 4

Briefly outline the pathway from grass roots level to Olympic squad in France.

Exam questions   answers: page 122

1   Describe how the French government takes an active role in supporting and promoting both mass participation and élite sport in France.

(15 minutes)

2   Describe the structure and function of sports study sections in France.

(8 minutes)

Answers
The comparative study of global sporting systems

Sport in North American cultures

Checkpoints

1 The rags to riches ideal can be achieved through sport in the USA. A performer can start playing in a little league and work their way up to the professional ranks and become a millionaire sports star.
2 Endorsement is where a sports star allows a company to use their name on the company's products.
3 Funding available for sport in the USA comes from commercial sponsorship, merchandising, media fees, gate receipts and private investors.
4 American football reflects the culture of the USA in that it is a very sophisticated and technical game with a large division of labour with very specialist positions, it is also high scoring and entertaining.

Exam question

The historical and cultural reasons to explain why the USA holds 'world championships' in sports which only Americans compete in are: the USA has a long history of independence, a period of state-led isolation coincided with the rational phase of sports development. Most sports competitions in the USA developed at this time, and the huge size and variety of states led to a high level of competition. Big-four sports in the USA are so far ahead that there is no point in any other nations competing.

Administration of sport in North American cultures

Checkpoints

1 Autonomous means self-governing, independent.
2 Title IX legislates against gender discrimination in sport in USA educational institutions.
3 Booster clubs are community clubs made up of old boys and local businessmen who help support financially school and college teams.
4 The draft system attempts to reflect the American ideal of the land of opportunity in that the worst team gets the first pick, so in theory every team at the start of each season should have an equal opportunity to win.

Exam question

Some reasons for the huge community interest and support for high-school sport in America are: huge distance between professional teams; schools give a place to socialise for US communities; schools acts as nurseries for élite sport; stadia and facilities are of a very high standard; school sport is followed by the media.

Mass participation and élite sport in the USA

Checkpoints

1 The term professional franchise means a business agreement set up to maximise profit.

2 Little league competition in the USA mirrors the professional sports scene because it follows the conference and play model that all professional sports do, the equipment and uniforms are scaled-down versions of the adult game, the underlying ethic is still to win.
3 Counter-culture is one that goes against the mainstream, in the USA this is manifest in the recreational ethic, that is, taking part is more important than winning.
4 The media funds sport in the USA, controls the timing of sports events, advertises and promotes sports, and increasingly owns sports clubs.

Exam question

The USA is an élitist society where the drive is to be successful and win, playing sport at a lower level can be seen as wasting one's energy which would be better focussed on gaining the American dream. The decentralised and private-sector-dominated sports scene also means there are few opportunities both in terms of clubs and facilities to participate at local level.

Sport in New World culture – Australia

Checkpoints

1 Having a 'youthful' population is an advantage in terms of international sporting success because it means there is a large pool to select from, sport is mainly a young person's activity.
2 The transportation system aided the development of Australia because it meant that Britain could quickly populate the new continent and use the prisoners to build the infrastructure.
3 Australia's colonial history is reflected in the sports they play as they tend to play sports that originated in the UK. Australia has really adapted one sport only – Australian rules, from rugby. Recently immigration from southern Europe has led to an increase in the scope and popularity of soccer.
4 Being a member of the Commonwealth maintains a link between Australia and the UK because the queen remains the head of state and there are still close links between the two governments. It also allows both countries to compete in the Commonwealth Games.

Exam question

Outdoor sport in Australia is popular in schools due to the closeness of the outback to most population centres and the need to teach young people about the dangers and survival techniques. Outdoor pursuits are also a good way of using a free resource around most schools.

Outdoor sport is popular among Australian communities due to the accessibility of the outback and beach, temperate weather suits outdoor activity and also reflects on the pioneering tradition of the country.

Administration of sport in Australia

Checkpoints

1 The term federal, in the context of governance, relates to the national or commonwealth government. Australia also has separate state governments.
2 Australia's sport follows a decentralised system. Each state has its own independent department of sport and recreation that takes responsibility for all levels of sport in their state. The ASC does attempt to coordinate sports policy across Australia.
3 Each state is responsible for the structure and content of PE programmes in Australia and has its own education department which works closely with the state department of sport and recreation to coordinate PE programmes across their own state.
4 The Fundamental Motor Skills Programme's aims are the identification of key motor skills for adult sports. These are taught to all school pupils in order to give a 'fair go for all' in sport.

Exam question

The structure and philosophy of the Sports Education programme includes: compulsory sports lessons for all separate from PE to give all pupils a chance to participate in sport on a regular basis; season of sport runs in each term based on internal competition; students run the sessions – coaching and officiating; gives an opportunity to take part in sport's wider roles rather than just performing.

Mass participation and élite sport in Australia

Checkpoints

1 Active Australia is about promoting healthy lifestyles through participation in regular physical activity.
2 Natural and cultural advantages that Australia has over the UK are: Australia has greater spaces for sport, a young population and a more favourable climate.
3 Geographical factors that may limit the scope of professional sport in Australia are the large distances between capital cities where most teams are based.
4 The AIS reflects the decentralising factors of the separate states in Australia because each state has its own institute of sport offering support for élite athletes in that state.

Exam question

Strategies that Australia has used in an attempt to establish Olympic success are: after 1976 a network of sports institutes was set up offering support and facilities for the top athletes. Élite athletes get sports science support; state grants to allow full-time training; medal winners are offered financial rewards; the sports search programme identifies potential talent; widening participation means a larger pool of talent.

Sport in France

Checkpoints

1 The type of sports that suit France's rural nature are: individual sports and those that use the natural environment as a resource: cycling, hunting, skiing, walking and climbing.
2 In terms of administration centralised means that the power and administration comes from one source, in the case of France the control of sport is soley in the hands of the central government.
3 President de Gaulle believed that sporting success could be used as a form of nation building and as a tool to revitalise the French spirit.
4 The position of Sports Minister in France and in the UK differs in that the Sports Minister in France takes a central role in the control of sport whereas in the UK the position has only limited responsibility for the control and administration of sport.

Exam question

The reasons behind the French government's support of sport at all levels is that the government believes that the sporting success can bring national pride and a feel-good factor to the population. Promoting mass participation can bring about improved health, social inclusion and economic benefits. The Olympic failure of 1976 led to a review of policy and the state took control.

PE and school sport in France

Checkpoints

1 The 'tier temps pedagogique' programme divides up the primary curriculum into three equal parts: social, academic and physical. It should result in primary schools offering six hours of physical education per week.
2 The three types of transplant classes are: ski class, sea class and countryside class.
3 The conflict that better school-age performers have on Wednesday afternoons is that Wednesday afternoon sport is aimed at mass participation. Consequently more able performers will compete for, and train at, sporting clubs that also run their junior programmes on Wednesday afternoons.
4 The role of the sports study sections is that they act as regional centres for the teaching and training of élite young sports performers.

Exam question

Examples of central control within the French education system are: all schools follow the same timetable, all having

Wednesday afternoon off. All subjects are taught in the same way. The official instruction says exactly what has to be taught in each lesson. All students take the same multi-subject exam.

Mass participation and élite sport in France

Checkpoints

1 The transplant class system in French schools helps promote mass participation by teaching young people a range of outdoor sports that will hopefully encourage them to keep on participating in their adult life.
2 The aim of the national plan was to provide enough sports equipment and facilities to meet the needs of the whole population.
3 The topography and culture of France is suited to the ideal of rustic simplicity because France is a large country with a rural focus. Agriculture is still a very important industry and a good communication and transport network means the countryside is accessible. France is blessed with a wide range of different terrains.
4 The pathway from grass roots level to the Olympic squad in France is: skills learnt at primary school → Wednesday afternoon sport → sports study section through UNSS or clubs → CREPS (Regional sports academy → INSEP → Olympic squad

Exam questions

1 The French sports system is a centralised one, the Department for Youth and Sport takes a coordinator role in both élite and mass sport. The government funds and supports the élite network and the national academy for sport, INSEP. The government funds élite performers in terms of their training and also offers rewards to athletes who win medals.

   Sport pour tous is a national programme supported by the government that promotes mass participation.
2 The structure and function of the sports study sections in France is that they have a mission to develop excellence, similar to sports schools in the UK. They operate within conventional schools but select children with high sporting potential. Although sporting talent is important, so too is academic progress. Training schedules are arranged around timetabled study and specialist coaches work with children. They receive direct government funding.

Revision checklist
The comparative study of global sporting systems

1	Give an overview of sport in the USA	Confident	Not confident. **Revise** pages 102–103
2	Explain how sport is administered in the USA	Confident	Not confident. **Revise** pages 104–105
3	Describe the historical development of sport and PE in the USA	Confident	Not confident. **Revise** pages 102–103
4	Comment on the concept of mass participation in the USA	Confident	Not confident. **Revise** pages 106–107
5	Explain the structure of élite sport in the USA	Confident	Not confident. **Revise** pages 106–107
6	Give an overview of sport in Australia	Confident	Not confident. **Revise** pages 108–109
7	Describe the historical development of Australian sport and PE	Confident	Not confident. **Revise** pages 108–109
8	Explain how sport is administered in Australia	Confident	Not confident. **Revise** pages 110–111
9	Describe the structure and function of school and college sport in Australia	Confident	Not confident. **Revise** pages 110–111
10	Comment on the concept of mass participation in Australia	Confident	Not confident. **Revise** pages 112–113
11	Explain the structure of élite sport in Australia	Confident	Not confident. **Revise** pages 112–113
12	Describe the cultural background of Australian sport	Confident	Not confident. **Revise** pages 108–109
13	Give an overview of sport in France	Confident	Not confident. **Revise** pages 114–115
14	Describe the historical development of French sport and PE	Confident	Not confident. **Revise** pages 114–115
15	Explain how sport is administered in France	Confident	Not confident. **Revise** pages 114–115
16	Describe the structure and function of school and college sport in France	Confident	Not confident. **Revise** pages 116–117
17	Comment on the concept of mass participation in France	Confident	Not confident. **Revise** pages 118–119
18	Explain the structure of élite sport in France	Confident	Not confident. **Revise** pages 118–119

This section is intended to help you develop your study skills for examination success. You will benefit if you try to develop skills from the beginning of your course. Modern AS and A-level exams are not just tests of your recall of textbooks and your notes. Examiners who set and mark the papers are guided by assessment objectives that include skills as well as knowledge.

Exam board specifications

In order to organise your notes and revision you will need a copy of your exam board's syllabus specification. You can obtain a copy by writing to the board or by downloading the syllabus from the exam board's website.

AQA (Assessment and Qualifications Alliance)
Publications Department, Stag Hill House, Guildford, Surrey
GU2 5XJ
www.aqa.org.uk

EDEXCEL
190 High Holburn, London WC1V 7BH
www.edexcel.org.uk

OCR (Oxford, Cambridge and Royal Society of Arts)
1 Hills Road, Cambridge CB2 1GG
www.ocr.org.uk

WJEC (Welsh Joint Education Committee)
245 Western Avenue, Cardiff CF5 2YX
www.wjec.co.uk

The AS/A-level specifications

All A-level courses are in two parts, with a number of separate modules or units in each part. Students will start by studying the AS (Advanced Subsidiary). Those wishing to do so will go on to study the second part of the course, called A2. There is some element of choice as to which modules are studied but this may depend on the awarding body.

Action point

Check with your teacher how your practical sports skills will be asessed.

The jargon

Every A-level specification includes *synoptic assessment* at the end of the A2 course. Synoptic questions draw on the ideas and concepts of earlier units and thus link topics. Synoptic assessment is dealt with in more detail on pages 128 to 129.

Advanced subsidiary

The AS modules are compulsory and they cover the common core of the subject. AS is designed to provide appropriate assessment of knowledge, understanding and skills expected of candidates who have completed the first half of a full A-level qualification. The level of demand of the AS exam is that expected of candidates halfway through a full A-level course of study, i.e. between GCSE and A level.

AS may be used in one of two ways:

→ As a final qualification, allowing you to broaden your studies and to defer a decision about specialism.
→ As the first half (50 per cent) of an A-level qualification which must be completed before an A-level award can be made.

Thus the AS specification establishes core principles on which an understanding of physical education and sport is based, and at the same time covers relevant topics in sufficient depth to form coherent modules for students who may not continue their study of physical education and sport to A level.

A level (AS + A2)

The A-level exam course is in two parts:

→ The AS is the first half of the course and constitutes 50 per cent of the total award. It will normally comprise three teaching and learning modules or units.
→ The A2 is the second half of the course, the remaining 50 per cent of the total award. It also normally comprises a further three teaching and learning modules or units which, in addition to introducing new knowledge, extends the core principles.

Each teaching and learning module will normally be assessed through an associated assessment unit.

Assessment units

AS and A2 physical education and sport each comprise six assessment units or modules. In both AS and A2 two of the units are assessed by written examination taken at two specific times of the year, January and June. The third component in each case involves a method of practical assessment. Awarding Bodies use a combination of centre-assessed coursework and moderated practical sports assessment.

What are the main differences between AS and A2?

→ AS and A2 courses are designed so that the level of difficulty steadily increases, with the A2 containing the more demanding concepts.
→ In A2 there is much greater emphasis on the skills of application and analysis than in AS.
→ A2 includes synoptic assessment.

Modules and their shelf life

Any module can be retaken to improve your grade. You may resit any unit once during the time when the results are held in the Awarding Body's unit bank. When you decide to cash in for an AS/A-level award the Awarding Body will use the best result from each unit you have attempted. Any AS result can be converted into a full A-level award by taking the A2 exam at any time while the specification remains valid.

Assessment objectives

For AS and A level the scheme of assessment will test your ability in the following areas:

→ knowledge and understanding
→ application of knowledge and understanding, analysis, synthesis and evaluation
→ experiment and investigation
→ quality of written communication.

At A2 there is an additional category: synthesis of knowledge, understanding and skills. This is the synoptic element, where knowledge and skills from different modules are linked together and assessed.

Action point

Not all A2 units are assessed in the January series of exams, check with your teacher how and when you will be assessed.

Examiner's secrets

The examination specification (formerly called the syllabus) is an extremely *useful* document. It clearly states the requirements for each topic you study. You should obtain your own copy, from your teacher, the Internet, or by application to the relevant examination board (known as the Awarding Body). If you are not sure which Awarding Body to contact, your teacher will be able to help you.

Links

While the content of each of the modules at AS is self-contained, during the study of each module, opportunities should be taken to enable you to integrate different aspects of the subject. The link feature helps you to achieve this by highlighting connections between different chapters in the revision guide. The specification is designed to allow for the progression from AS to A level, both in terms of the difficulty of the topics and in the skill and understanding that are required.

Synoptic assessment

One of the aims of A2 assessment is to enable candidates to show knowledge and understanding of facts, principles and concepts from different areas of physical education and to make connections between them. You must understand what is meant by 'synoptic assessment' if you are to be fully prepared for your A2 examinations.

Synoptic assessment

Involves the drawing together of knowledge, understanding and skills learnt in the different units of AS/A2 physical education course.

→ It may require you to apply knowledge of a number of areas of the course to a particular situation or context.
→ It may require you to use knowledge and understanding of principles and contexts in planning experimental work and in the analysis and evaluation of data.
→ It will take place at the end of your course.

Why do A2 exams contain a synoptic element?

Modular exams were introduced for a variety of reasons, one of which was to allow students to study a 'theme' in a manageable block of information.

However, in a modular course there is a tendency for candidates to gain success in a unit then forget the concepts they have learnt as soon as the exam has been taken.

Synoptic questions require you to transfer concepts from one unit to another and make connections.

Having an overview of the subject is thought to be a better preparation for higher education and employment.

Being able to link information gives you a greater understanding and is more satisfying and fulfilling, allowing you to contribute more effectively in problem-solving situations.

How can I gain synoptic skills?

Physical education is inherently cyclical and therefore synoptic in the world of sport coaches, managers and teachers who are constantly looking at many different ways of improving performance. You will have naturally applied many of these ideas and skills learnt during AS physical education and even your GCSE course! So in studying A2 physical education you will have been using synoptic skills without realising it.

Examiner's secrets

Part of your physical education course is assessed using synoptic questions. These are written so that you can draw together knowledge and understanding and skills learnt in different parts of AS and A2 physical education.

Examiner's secrets

Don't be phased by synoptic questions. The examiner will not expect you to memorise specific detailed information from a previous unit studied but rather will expect you to use concepts that you have acquired to make links.

Action point

Check the specification with your teacher and look at past papers to determine the type of synoptic questions you can expect.

How can I prepare for synoptic questions?

→ From your specification check out which module will contain synoptic questions.
→ Revise the basics of earlier modules and as you do so list topics that link with those you have recently studied at A2.
→ Carry out regular revision throughout the course.
→ Make use of past question papers, particularly specimen questions provided by your Awarding Body.
→ As you can expect to encounter new contexts which draw together different ideas, read generally around the subject and 'check the net'.

How are synoptic questions marked

Examiners use the following criteria when they asses your synoptic answers:

→ **Practical links and examples** – try and back up each point you make with a specific sports example, the more detail the better.
→ **Theoretical links** – make as many references to named theories and research you have covered in all the modules you have studied.
→ **Analysis** – show that you understand the topic area, debate and challenge the issue in the question.
→ **Opinion and judgement** – don't be afraid to give your own feeling on the subject, you can relate an answer to your own experience in sport.
→ **Use of technical language** – try to incorporate as many technical terms as you can so long as they apply to the topic area. Don't forget to also include a definition or explanation of the terms you use.

Action point

As you review your notes make your own synoptic links.

Action point

Try and pick out the main synoptic topics for your specification. Produce and use a set of revision cards that answer the following points:
→ How does this issue/topic link to the other topics I have studied?
→ Can I link any theories, perspectives or research to this topic?
→ Can I identify a debate about this issue/topic?
→ Can I refer to specific examples or case studies linked to this issue/topic?

Study skills

This spread gives advice on taking notes during your studies and revision techniques to help you prepare for your exams.

Note taking

Note taking involves condensing speech or writing into an abbreviated form, which nevertheless contains the same essential information as the original. This is a skill, particularly important in the study of physical education and sport where there is a wide range of topics and subjects. The process of note taking requires you to concentrate on the essential information and in itself is an aid to learning. The second function of note taking is to provide you with an aid to future study and revision. It is much easier to refer back to and revise from notes that you have made yourself.

If you are a student attending classes you will probably make most of your notes during lessons and lectures, with your teacher being the main source of information. There are two pitfalls you must try to avoid: do not try to take down every word the teacher says, and when making notes from written sources do not copy out whole passages. The purpose of note taking is to produce a more manageable summary of the most important information.

The following are some points of general advice:

→ Use a looseleaf file so that you can add to or arrange your notes.
→ Space your notes out on the page so that you can add further information later.
→ Pick out key words or headings by underlining or using a highlighter pen.
→ Always write down book and page references in case you need to check back at a latter date, course work assessment usually includes marks for including a reference section.
→ Don't forget to include quotes and the names of theories you come across.
→ Consider diagrams and flow charts as an alternative way of presenting information.

Reading

A-level success depends partly upon the ability to acquire and retain a wide range of knowledge. This is most effectively achieved by reading around the subject; class notes and a textbook alone are inadequate. Try to use more than one textbook as authors vary in their treatment of topics. There are also a number of excellent television programmes and video presentations on many of the topics covered in physical education and sport and these can also be useful sources of additional information.

Action point

Make your own notes from several sources. Authors vary in the depth of treatment of topics, therefore it is advisable to read a range of publications.

Examiner's secrets

Teachers recommend using more than one of your senses to aid learning. That's why they often combine talk and chalk with other visual material such as worksheets, TV, etc. Think about using graphic representations of knowledge.

Examiner's secrets

Read around the subject. This increases your vocabulary and grammar.

Active revision

Start revising in good time; it will allow you to practise and develop the necessary skills to use in the exam. If you are studying other subjects, devise a plan where you use set times to study each subject.

Try and identify what you need to revise in terms of skills as well as topics. Completing a series of practise questions, such as those included in the guide, can be a good starting point in identifying any areas that you need to work on. Plan your revision on a week-by-week basis.

Review your plan regularly and adapt it as necessary. Some topics and activities will take more or less time than you anticipated. Build in opportunities for relaxation and fun in your schedule; breaks for fresh air and exercise will help your concentration.

Revision strategies

Use tables – these can help you organise information so that it can be used in different ways.

Discuss issues in your class

→ Have question and answer sessions with fellow students.
→ Ask a family member to test you on the key words for each unit.
→ Make audio tapes of key points and theories which you can play back when you are sitting on the bus or on your way to class – there is always time for revision!

Active revision – use examination questions

After you have revised a topic area it is vital that you are able to apply your knowledge and understanding in a critical way to an examination question. Whole questions may appear daunting at first. Try answering the shorter sub-questions or writing plans for the essay and synoptic questions.

The benefits of using real questions

→ You become familiar with the style and language used in questions.
→ There will be popular questions which examine similar areas, even if the precise wording changes.
→ They provide a check on your understanding as well as your recall of knowledge.
→ They may reveal gaps in your knowledge and weaknesses in one or more topic areas; use this feedback to review your revision plan.
→ You can practise doing difficult questions.

Examiner's secrets

Tackle an unfamiliar question by applying your knowledge of relevant theories.

Action point

Check out your examination board's website, most include specimen exam papers and mark schemes which you can download.

Exam papers

At both AS and A level there is a considerable emphasis on understanding, interpreting and applying knowledge. In addition to the factual content, you will need to appreciate the underlying principles and apply these to sporting situations. This, and the information below, will better prepare you for the types of questions you will encounter on exam papers. It will also enable you to understand the principles involved.

Exam questions

Each module or unit will contain a number of structured questions, some may also require you to answer a longer question or essay, this is often true of the A2 papers. There may be a choice of questions but no more than one or two per module. Examiners spend a considerable amount of time preparing, revising and refining exam questions. The contents of each paper are agreed upon by a committeee after each question has undergone a thorough and rigorous analysis to minimise the chance of misinterpretation by the student.

During revision, when confronted with a mass of information, it is tempting to try and work out which topics are 'going to come up' and not revise certain topics. This is not a good idea with modular exams as the questions are designed to cover every topic outlined on the specification. You should be asking yourself what you should do with the knowledge that you have.

Structured questions

These are the most common types of questions used in AS and A-level physical education and sport exams. They usually require you to write at least a number of short sentences, although can also include the opportunity for extended writing.

Remember that the mark allocation given to each question is a good guide in terms of how much the examiners are expecting you to write. Some exam boards also combine the question and answer paper together and the space available for the answer to a question is another good indicator of how much writing you need to include in your answers.

Structured questions are often presented in several parts based around a common topic area. You may well experience an increase in the degree of difficulty as you work through the questions. The first part may be simple recall, perhaps defining a term. The most difficult part is often at the end and may ask you to give an opinion or analysis about an issue in physical education and sport. Very often in physical

---

Action point

Do rough calculations of how much time to spend on questions for the papers you are sitting. Use these time allocations when practising answers and develop a confident view of how much you can write in that time.

Examiner's secrets

Examiners do not set out to trick you. Very often candidates may panic or not read the question sufficiently carefully, and so trick themselves.

Watch out!

Papers have inbuilt time for you to read the question carefully. This enables you to decide on which topic the question is focussing and highlight key words.

Watch out!

Where you have choice always read through the whole of the question before deciding if that is the one for you.

education and sports questions marks will be awarded for referring to practical sports examples, many questions will actually state this, but it is good practice to try and back up any factual points you make with a practical sports example.

Essay and higher mark questions

All too often students rush into essay and higher mark questions, writing everything they know about the topic identified in the question. You need to take time with this type of question, first reading the question through several times to ensure you understand fully what it is that you are required to do. When you start such a question, plan or sketch out your answer, this will not only help you organise your answer logically but will also give you a checklist to which you can refer while writing out your final answer. In this way you will be less likely to repeat yourself, wander off the subject or miss out important sections.

Very often essay and higher mark questions in physical education and sport will require debate or discussion of an issue. The trick here is to look to develop two sides of an argument. Sometimes the argument required will be clearly evident in the question set, in others you may have the choice and need to develop your own debate.

A basic plan that could be used to answer an essay or higher mark could include the following:

→ **Intro** – set out how you are going to answer the question that the examiners have set.
→ **Key terminolgy** – introduce any key terms or theories you think relate to the question.
→ **Overview** – outline a basic background to the topic area. In a social cultural question this could include an historical overview of the issue. In a scientific question this may include an overview of the relevant theories and research.
→ **Case study/applied example** – can you relate the question to a specific practical sports example or specific case study or investigation you have covered?
→ **Answer specific points** – does the question ask you to discuss and explain any areas in particular?
→ **Conclusion** – sum up the main points you have made in your answer, can you finish with a personal opinion or view?

Exam papers (continued)

Key words in examinations

Exam questions use various words that key you in to how to approach them. A list of the words frequently used in exam questions, together with their approximate meanings, is given below.

Brief: A short statement of only the main points.

Calculate: Work out, showing all the stages in the derivation of the answer (your workings).

Compare: Write about the similarities and differences between two different topics or systems, e.g. school sport in one country compared to another named culture.

Define: State the meaning of, for example, a term without actually using the term itself.

Describe: A request for factual detail about a structure or process expressed logically and concisely.

Discuss: A critical account of various viewpoints and arguments in the topic set, drawing attention to their relative importance and significance. For example: discuss the advantages and disadvantages of a dedicated sports school system.

Evaluate: A judgement of evidence and/or arguments is required.

Explain: Describe and give reasons for.

Graphs: When a graph is being interpreted it is essential to relate any changes or trends. To plot a graph would require graph paper and some degree of accuracy. To sketch a graph requires only a rough outline.

Identify: Requires a word, phrase or brief statement. Show you recognise a concept or a theory in an item.

Illustrate: Include diagrams or drawings as much as possible or may also be linked to a specific practical example.

List: A sequence of numbered points one below the other with no further explanation.

Outline: Give only the main points. This means 'don't go into detail'. But if you have learnt the topic thoroughly you may be tempted to waste time by writing too much!

State: A brief concise answer giving no reasons.

Suggest: There may be more than one explanation but as long as yours is reasonable it will gain some marks. This means that the question has no fixed answer and a wide range of reasonable responses is acceptable.

What is meant by: A definition is usually required. The amount of information to be included is dictated by the mark value.

Using past questions

You should make use of past papers, set by the Awarding Body whose exams you are taking, as preparation for your exams. Your school or college may provide you with past papers or you can write to the relevant Awarding Body or check out their website. Awarding Bodies also publish the mark schemes used by the examiners. These serve as an excellent guide to what is required on any particular topic.

At the end of each spread in this study guide there are exam questions, and the model answer to each question is given at the end of each section. You should attempt each question without reference to your notes, taking notice of the time allocation. After completing the question, mark it yourself. Your wording may not be quite the same but should contain the key words identified in the answer scheme. If you have not achieved a satisfactory answer, don't be too despondent. Check your notes and rewrite your answer. This way you will improve your understanding and learn from your mistakes. You will probably remember the right answer much better for having gone over it again.

Know the bodies and agencies that influence

It is useful to be able to include in your exam answers examples and facts about the various bodies that influence sport in the UK, many of the questions in the socio-cultural units may ask direct questions about these bodies.

British Association of Sport and Exercise Sciences – aims to promote scientific study of sport and exercise in the UK.
More info: www.bases.org.uk

British Olympic Association – the national Olympic committee for Great Britain and Northern Ireland, they select and manage the Olympic teams as well as encourage participation at all levels and further the Olympic ideals within the country.
More info: www.boa.org.uk

British Paralympic Association – selects funds and manages Great Britain's Paralympic team for the Paralympic Games. It is a registered charity whose core purpose is to create the best possible environment in which Britain's competitors can produce their lifetime's best performances.
More info: www.paralympics.org.uk

British Sports Trust – uses sport to develop skills for life through its Sports Leaders Awards, there are three awards specifically in sport and a fourth in basic expedition leadership.
More info: www.bst.org.uk

Central Council of Physical Recreation – acts as the voice of the national governing and representing bodies of sport and recreation in the UK. Speaks and acts to promote, protect and develop the interests of sport and physical recreation at all levels.
More info: www.ccpr.org.uk

Department for Education and Skills – the UK government department with responsibility for education including PE and sport in schools.
More info: www.dfes.gov.uk

Department of Culture, Media and Sport – the UK government department whose responsibility includes promoting and supporting all levels of sport and recreation.
More info: www.culture.gov.uk

English Federation of Disability Sport – the voice of disability sport in England. Launched in October 1999 it is the umbrella organisation for disabled sportsmen and women in the country. The EFDS seeks to represent all disabled people and works closely with the seven National Disability Sports Organisations (NDSOs).
More info: www.efds.co.uk

sport and recreation in the United Kingdom

Institute of Leisure and Amenity Management (ILAM) – is the professional body for the leisure industry and represents the interests of leisure managers across all sectors and specialisms of leisure.
More info: www.ilam.co.uk

National Coaching Foundation – the old name for SportCoach UK.

National Council for School Sport (NCSS) – the voice of school sport. The NCSS is a national forum body for school sport associations and others with an interest in school sport. Its main aim is to promote school sport opportunities for young people.
More info: www.ncss.org.uk

National Playing Fields Association (NPFA) – campaigns and promotes the protection of playing fields across the UK.
More info: www.npfa.co.uk

SportAid (formerly known as the Sports Aid Foundation) – set up in 1998 and funded by the Foundation for Sport and the Arts, much of their funds come from the football pools. The organisation gives grants to developing athletes who are outside the World Class Programme.
More info: www.sportsaid.org.uk

Sport England – is the lead sports development agency for England and the major distributor of the National Lottery sports fund. Its aim is to foster a healthier and more successful nation through increased investment in sport and active recreation. Other examples would include Sports Scotland, Sport Cymru and the Northern Ireland Sports Council.
More info: www.sportengland.org.uk

Women's Sport Foundation (WSF) – funded through the sports councils, its aim is to promote female involvement in sport at all levels. It runs schemes to encourage female participants as well as raising the profile of élite female performers.
More info: www.wsf.org.uk

Youth Sports Trust – a registered charity established in 1994 with the aim of building a brighter future for young people in sport. Its main influence has been through the management of TOPs and Millennium Volunteer Programmes. It also supports schools that have specialist sport college status and those involved in the school sport coordinators programme.
More info: www.youthsporttrust.org

Know the strategies and schemes that affect sport

It is useful to be able to include in your exam answers examples and facts about the various schemes and strategies that have been introduced to support sport and recreation in the UK, many of the questions in the socio-cultural units may ask direct questions about these bodies.

ACE UK – (Athlete Career and Education Services) part of the World Class Programme coordinated by UK Sport and the sports councils which aims to maximise career and educational opportunities for élite athletes while they are preparing for global competition.

Activemark – an award scheme for primary schools which recognises good practice in physical education.

Active Schools Programme – part of Sport England's Active Sports Programme (see below), it gives a quality framework for schools in their delivery of PE and sporting opportunities. The main focus of the programme are awards Activemark and Sportsmark schools can apply for.

Active Sports Programme – *more people, more places, more medals* – is the main focus of Sport England at the start of the twenty-first century. The aim of the scheme is to promote active recreation at community and schools level with the hope that this in turn will increase world-class achievement. Most of the funding for the programmes has been raised through the National Lottery.
More info: wwwsportengland.org.uk

Champion Coaching – part of the National Junior Sports Programme. Its aim is to give talented young sports performers access to quality coaching facilitated by the NCF (now Sports Coach UK).

Coach Development Officers Programme (CDOs) – £4 million worth of funding from the UK government has enabled Sports Coach UK to create CDO positions across UK to gain recognition of coaching as a profession with accredited qualifications and a real career development structure.
More info: www.sportcoach.org.uk

Dragon Sport – a Sports Council Wales initiative that aims to recruit volunteers to provide extracurricular sports sessions for children, it is supported by the Youth Sport Trust and follows a similar model to the TOPS scheme.

English Institute of Sport – is a network of centres and service providers aiming to provide the best high-performance training environment in the world, for world-class programme athletes.

FA Charter Standard Awards – a kitemarking scheme that establishes the minimum standards of football development in schools. Schools need to attain FA qualifications for teachers, provide football for boys and girls within the curriculum and out of hours as well as linking to a junior club to allow children to extend their participation.
More info: www.thefa.com/grassroots/footballinschools

Gifted and Talented Programme – UK government programme launched in September 2003, was a national scheme to identify and support school pupils who were gifted in a number of areas including sport.

Millennium Volunteers Programme – Millennium Volunteers (MV) is aimed at young people aged 16–24. As an MV you volunteer your time to help others by doing something you enjoy. Many projects have a specific focus on sport and recreation.

National Junior Sports Programmes – launched in 1996 by Sport England and YST. Its aim is to encourage young people in sport through a series of linked programmes:

Top play – aimed at 4–9 yrs – learning basic movement skills in a fun way.

Top sport – aimed at 7–11 yrs – mini-games that develop sport skills.

Champion coaching – see above.

Top Club – aimed at 11+ yrs – specialising in a specific sport.

PESSCL – PE, School Sport and Club Links strategy whose aim is to increase to 75 per cent the proportion of 5- to 16-year-old children who spend a minimum of two hours each week on high-quality PE and sport within the curriculum.

More info: www.teachernet.gov/pe

Playing for Success – a DfES scheme that established out of hours study support centres in sports clubs and grounds, mainly aimed at professional football clubs.

More info: wwwdfes.gov.uk/playingforsuccess

Project Oarsome – a project that followed the success of GB rowers at the Olympics. A programme under the National Junior Rowing Programme with the aim of promoting, developing and sustaining participants in the sport of rowing.

Schools Partnerships Programme – launched in September 2000 as part of the UK government's PE and school sport strategy, it was originally called the School Sports Co-ordinator Programme.

School Sport Co-ordinator Programme – has been jointly funded by the DfES, DCMS, New Opportunities Fund and YST to improve sports provision in local communities. Now part of the **SPP** programme (see above).

Sportmark – a national award, presented by Sport England, to schools that can demonstrate a commitment to PE and sport and that work in partnership with their local community to provide a range of out-of-school-hours activities.

Step into Sport – a leadership and volunteering project jointly managed by Sport England, the British Sport Trust and the Youth Sports Trust in response to the UK government's plan for sport – *A Sporting Future for All* published March 2001. The main focus of the scheme is to develop leadership and volunteering in sport for young people aged 14 to 25 and older adults (50+).

Talented Athlete Scholarship Scheme (TASS) – coordinated by DCMS offering a range of scholarships and bursaries to promising sports stars aged 16 to 25. The pot of £6 million will be used to give identified athletes access to quality coaching, physiotherapy and facilities at the UKSIs.

Taylor Reports (1989 and 1990) – appointed by the UK government to inquire into the cause of and background to, the Hillsborough football disaster. Recommended a complete rethink of the safety and maintenance of sports grounds in Britain – specifically the introduction of all-seater stadiums.

TOP Link – encourages secondary school students to organise and run festivals of sport or dance for partner primary or special school pupils. TOP Link is also part of the Step into Sport programme that is designed to recruit, train, deploy and support young sports leaders.

Know the strategies and schemes and sports bodies

It is useful to be able to include in your exam answers examples and facts about the various bodies that influence sport globally, many of the questions in the socio-cultural units may ask direct questions about these bodies.

Able Aussie – target group programme coordinated by the ASC to raise the profile of disabled sport in Australia.

Active Australia – a national framework of mass participation, set up in 1916 and coordinated by the ASC.

Australian Council for Heath, Physical Education and Recreation – is a national professional association representing people who work in the areas of health education, physical education, recreation, sport, dance, community fitness or movement sciences. The mission of the council is to promote healthy lifestyles for all Australians and particularly to study and promote its areas of focus.
More info: www.achper.org.au

Australian Football League (AFL) – governing body of Australian Rules Football, Americanised in recent years through a franchise programme and annual draft.

Australian Institute of Sport – based in Canberra, the federal capital, and set up in 1981, creates a central training base for Australia's top athletes.

Australian Sports Commission – the body that coordinates sport across Australia, and is enriching the lives of all Australians through sport. It is responsible for both increasing participation and developing sports excellence in Australia.

Aussie Sport – a programme of sports with modified rules to encourage young people to participate in sporting activity.

Fundamental Motor Skills – a programme launched in the state of Victoria, Australia, it gave all primary school teachers access to a resource pack that taught young children 10 basic motor skills required for sport.

Indigenous Sports Programme – developed by the ASC in Australia to encourage more of the indigenous people to participate in active recreation. Major initiatives include the desert sport carnivals and the Arrafura Games.

that influence and affect sport in the cultures you have studied

INSEP – National Institute of Sports and Physical Education for French sport, based just outside Paris, provides élite training for performers, coaches and teachers.

Le Plein Air – a popular philosophy in France and one that permeates much of the sport for all and educational programmes.

Lifetime sport – American concept of promoting physical activity that can be carried on throughout life, often with the *Golden Olympics* programmes for older people evident in many of the US states.

NCAA – National Collegiate Athletic Association – the body responsible for inter-college sport in the USA, also coordinates the athletic scholarship programme.

SEPEP – the Sport Education in Physical Education Program is a curriculum model for use in school physical education programmes in Australia. SEPEP relies on teachers and students to create a particular form of social system within physical education lessons known as student-centred learning.

Sport Pours Tous – French sports system with a similar concept to Sport for All, aimed at improving the health of the nation.

Tiers Temps – programme found in French primary schools, where the curriculum is split into thirds: social, academic and physical, which should relate to a weekly programme of six hours of physical education.

Title IX – federal legislation in the USA that promotes equal opportunity in terms of gender in school and college sport.

Transplant Classes – outdoor experiences for children in French primary schools, usually takes the form of class de neige (ski classes) or class de mer (sea).

UNSS – National Union of School sport responsible for coordinating Wednesday afternoon sport in French schools (**USEP** is the equivalent body for primary schools in France).

USOC – United States Olympic Committee, the national Olympic committee for the USA. It selects and manages the Olympic teams as well as encouraging participation at all levels and furthering the Olympic ideals within the country, unique in that it does receive federal funding.

Glossary

Access – being able to take part in sport.

Adenosine triphosphate (ATP) – the basic unit of energy within the body. It is the end product of each of the three main energy systems.

Aerobic – requiring oxygen.

Agility – a fitness component that combines speed and flexibility.

All-or-none law – a neurone or muscle fibre either responds completely or not at all to a stimulus.

Americanisation – where American trends and attitudes invade traditional culture.

American Dream – the idea that in the USA anyone can rise from rags to riches.

Arousal – degree of mental readiness before a performance.

Autonomous phase – the final stage of skill development where all performance skills are mastered and other performance factors can be practised.

Axon – nerve fibre carrying messages away from the nerve cell body.

Blood doping – an illegal ergogenic aid where athletes withdraw a quantity of blood some weeks before a competition and then re-inject this blood just before competition.

Booster clubs – community clubs made up of old boys and local businessmen that help support financially school and college teams.

Boycott – the refusal of a country to compete in an event, usually for political reasons.

Broken time payments – clubs paid working-class players the wages they could not earn while playing.

Capillaries – microscopic blood vessels that deliver oxygenated blood to the tissues via diffusion.

Capillarisation – the development of the capillary network in a part of the body, would include increasing the absolute number of capillaries and the capillary density.

Carbohydrate loading – diet manipulation aimed at increasing the muscles' glygogen stores before a sports event.

Cardiac output – the amount of blood pumped by the heart per minute.

Centre of gravity – the point around which the various body parts can be said to be in balance.

Coactors – individuals performing the same task, but independently.

Cognitive phase – the first stage of skill development which covers task familiarisation and some basic practice.

Concentric – muscle contraction where the muscle creates force while shortening in length.

Cool-down – last stage of training and/or competition where the body should gradually reduce physical activity to resting levels.

Cue – a signal for some particular action, may be verbal, visual or kinaesthetic.

Displacement – the distance an object has moved in a given direction.

DOMS (delayed onset of muscle soreness) – condition affecting the muscle that results in localised pain following strenuous exercise.

Draft system – the system where professional teams select the best college players once a year.

Eccentric – a muscle creating force while the fibres are lengthening.

EPOC (excess post-exercise oxygen consumption) – the extra oxygen needed to restore the body to its pre-exercise state.

Ergogenic aid – any method employed by an athlete to improve their performance.

Fatigue – depletion of the body's energy stores.

Franchise – a business agreement set up to maximise profit.

Glucose – the simplest form of carbohydrate and the basic ingredient for anaerobic and aerobic glycolysis.

Glycogen – the stored form of glucose, found in the muscles and liver.

Glycolysis the breakdown of glucose.

Hypertrophy – increase in muscle bulk due to an increase in the cross-sectional area of the muscle fibres.

Interval – a period of work in a training session.

Intrinsic – description of motives that lie within an individual's control.

Lactate – toxic by-product of anaerobic glycolysis.

Lombardian ethic – named after the famous Green Bay Packers' most successful coach Vince Lombardi, who developed the idea that winning is the most important thing.

Maximum oxygen uptake – the measure of the maximum amount of oxygen that the body can use for each kilogram of body weight in one minute, also referred to as VO_2max.

Mitochondria – the powerhouse of the cell where the Krebs cycle and electron transport system generates ATP.

Momentum – the product of mass and velocity ($M = mv$), it is a vector quantity and can be considered as a measure of the quantity of motion possessed by a body.

Motor unit – a nerve and its connecting muscle fibres.

Myoglobin – the oxygen-carrying agent within the muscle cell.

Onset of blood lactate accumulation (OBLA) – the point at which blood lactate levels suddenly increase, also referred to as lactate threshold.

PARQ – Physical Activity Readiness Questionnaire completed before training or testing to ensure that athletes are physiologically and psychologically prepared.

Peers – people who mix in the same environment, often of the same age.

Phosphocreatine – an energy-rich compound that is used by the body to create explosive energy.

Plyometrics – a method of fitness training that employs skipping and bounding actions to maximise power gains through isotonic eccentric muscle contractions.

Point of insertion – usually moves during muscle action.

Point of origin – remains relatively fixed during muscle action.

Proprioceptive neuromuscular facilitation (PNF) – usually performed with a partner and involves a pattern of alternating contraction and relaxation of the muscles being stretched.

Reaction time – the time taken to begin movement in response to a stimulus.

Recovery – the period following physical activity in which the body's systems repair damaged tissue and replenish energy stores.

Scalar quantity – physical quantity that is described completely in terms of its magnitude.

Schema – a mental framework or outline developed through past experience.

Self-efficacy – where an individual believes they have the ability to perform at a specified level in a certain task.

Significant other – a person who a performer relates to and holds in high esteem.

Social loafing – where an individual loses motivation within a group, linked to a loss of identity.

Target zone – a specific level of intensity that an athlete needs to work at to obtain a specific physiological adaptation.

Tidal volume – the amount of air moved each time we breathe, usually about 500ml.

Tier temps pedagogique 'A third time programme', where French primary schools are required to teach six hours of physical education a week.

Training zone – the zone within which it is necessary to have the heart rate to achieve a desired training effect.

Velocity – the rate at which a body moves, it is a vector quantity in that it possesses both magnitude and direction.

Vicarious experience – experiences gained by watching other people perform.

Vital capacity – the total amount of air that can be expired from the lungs after a maximum inhalation.

Further reading

General textbooks

Carnell, D., Ireland, J., et al. (2002) *Advanced PE for OCR AS* Heinemann
Honeybourne, J. (2003) *Btec National Sport* Nelson Thornes
Honeybourne, J., M. Hill and H. Moors (2004) *Advanced PE and Sport* 3rd Edn Nelson Thornes

Reference books

Adair, D. (1997) *Sport in Australian History*, Oxford University Press
Bailey, S. and W. Vamplew (1999) *100 Years of Physical Education 1899–1999* PEA
Clegg, C. (1995) *Exercise Physiology and Functional Anatomy* Feltham Press
Cox, R., G. Jarvie and W. Vamplew (2000) *Encyclopedia of British Sport* ABC-Clio
Danials, S. and A. Tedder (2000) *A Proper Spectacle – Women Olympians 1900–1936* ZeNaNa Press
Gill, D.L. (1986) *Psychological Dynamics of Sport* Human Kinetics
Gutmann, A. (1994) *The Olympics – A History of the Modern Games*, University of Illinois Press
Kent, M. (1998) *Oxford Dictionary of Sports Science and Medicine* 2nd Edn Oxford University Press
Money, T. (1987) *Manly and Muscular Diversions* The Bath Press
Schmidt, R.A. (1991) *Motor Learning and Performance* Human Kinetics
Seeley, R.R., Stephens, T.D. and P. Tate (1995) *Essentials of Anatomy and Physiology* Mosby
Sharp, R. (1992) *Acquiring Skill in Sport* Sports Dynamics
Wilmore, J.H. and D.L. Costhill (1999) *Physiology of Sport and Exercise* 2nd Edn Human Kinetics

Useful websites

www.ausport.gov.au
www.france.net
www.pe4u.co.uk
www.teachpe.com
www.physicaleducation.co.uk
www.uksport.gov.uk
www.youthsporttrust.org

This is not a prescriptive list and any further reading should be carried out after consultation with your teacher.

Index